The Boston Red Sox Killer B's

Baseball's Best Outfield

JIM PRIME AND BILL NOWLIN

Foreword by Fred Lynn
Afterword by Bob Costas

SPORTS
PUBLISHING

Sports Publishing books may be purchased in bulk at special discounts for sales promotion, corporate gifts, fund-raising, or educational purposes. Special editions can also be created to specifications. For details, contact the Special Sales Department, Sports Publishing, 307 West 36th Street, 11th Floor, New York, NY 10018 or sportspubbooks@skyhorsepublishing.com.

Sports Publishing® is a registered trademark of Skyhorse Publishing, Inc.®, a Delaware corporation.

Visit our website at www.sportspubbooks.com.

10 9 8 7 6 5 4 3 2 1

Library of Congress Cataloging-in-Publication Data is available on file.

Cover design by Tom Lau
Cover photo credit Getty Images

ISBN: 978-1-68358-338-7
Ebook ISBN: 978-1-68358-339-4

Printed in the United States of America

I dedicate this book to the 400-plus members of the Bluenose Bosox Brotherhood, an eclectic and informed group of Red Sox fans that recognizes no borders except foul lines, baselines, and outfield fences.
—Jim Prime

Dedicated to Red Sox fans worldwide. This has been quite a run, these past 15 years, hasn't it?
—Bill Nowlin

Contents

Foreword by Fred Lynn

For much of the 1970s, the Boston Red Sox trio of Jim Rice, Fred Lynn, and Dwight Evans comprised the best outfield in baseball. Many Red Sox historians and longtime fans also consider it the best outfield in Red Sox history. Center fielder Fred Lynn, former collegiate star at the University of Southern California, was the anchor of that outfield. The stylish left-hander exploded onto the major-league scene in 1975 along with fellow "Gold Dust Twin" Jim Rice.

He had a smooth, sweet swing and a presence in the outfield that reminded many of the great DiMaggio—Dom or Joe, take your pick. In his debut season, the 6-foot-1, 185-pound Lynn captured Rookie-of-the Year honors, was named American League MVP, and won a Gold Glove for his play in center field. He won three more Gold Gloves during his time in Boston and led the American League in batting in 1979 with a .333 average. Lynn was named to the American League All-Star team every season from 1975 to 1980. For the Sox, he batted .308 with 124 homers before moving on to the California Angels.

Who better to critique the current Red Sox outfield of Andrew Benintendi, Jackie Bradley Jr., and Mookie Betts than this legend, one of the most popular players ever to perform at Fenway? In this foreword and throughout the book, Lynn provides insights into his own Red Sox experience and offers a position-by-position commentary on the offensive and defensive strengths of his own classic outfield—and how they match up with the young challengers known as the Killer B's.

We call it the Big Stage, playing in New York, Philly, LA, and Boston. Some guys can play on the Big Stage and some can't. The Red Sox outfield of Andrew Benintendi, Jackie Bradley Jr., and Mookie Betts belong on the Big Stage.

There are similarities between the Jim Rice-Fred Lynn-Dwight Evans outfield of the 1970s and the Killer B's. We all arrived in the major leagues within a few years of each other and quickly became cohesive units. Like Jackie Jr., my counterpart in center field, I'd come from the college ranks. In fact, we are both USC alumni— for me, that stands for the University of Southern California; for him, the University of South Carolina. In left field, Benintendi is a compact, left-handed version of Jimmie. He's smaller, shorter, but he's got little Popeye arms, too. He's got some sock and he's got a short, compact swing—and he can go the other way pretty well. And in right field, both Dewey and Mookie can track down everything and get the ball back to the infield in a hurry. Both outfields had great confidence in their abilities and knew they could play in the majors from day one.

All three of the Killer B's are well-grounded. They come from good families that will make sure they stay that way. It looks like they do things together away from the ballpark, which is really nice to see. Two of them were college players and all three have handled the media extremely well. When I played, the Boston media used to be tough, but the Red Sox have now won four World Series in this century, one of which these three guys helped make happen so the pressure is now off. The pressure now is to repeat, but that's not the same thing as the pressure to win the first time. I mean, that's totally different.

Our games in the '70s were life and death every day. When we played the Yankees, there'd be 50 reporters in the locker room, either in New York or in Boston. You couldn't even get in there, there were so many. In Boston, I learned you speak when you're spoken to by the media and that's it. Don't volunteer anything. The middle '70s in Boston were some pretty tough times for the city. The pressure was ratcheted up. It was intense, like the cities themselves. Busing was a huge issue at that time and it was a rougher town, with places like the Combat Zone. It was a little sketchy going into that neighborhood. Nowadays that area almost looks like Disneyland to me compared to what it was then. Different times.

These guys don't feel the same kind of pressures today. They shouldn't, anyway. They've done it. They've won. Everybody's looking to knock them off now. People have to go through them to win the title.

Defensively, the biggest commonality about these guys is that all three can play center field. It gives them great flexibility, and to be honest it's a big advantage. If one center fielder goes down and can't play, they can fill it with a guy from either flank. That's a luxury we didn't have when we played together. I could play center, but with Jimmie and Dwight, that wasn't going to happen.

These three all have speed and that's why they can all play center. If you're going to compare the two outfields, that's where they are ahead of us: speed across the entire outfield. A pitcher's best friend is a fast outfield, so the Red Sox pitchers must love these guys. It certainly helps them at Fenway, but it really helps them on the road where you get more symmetrical ballparks and speed is definitely in play.

As far as their overall defensive ability is concerned, oh boy! You've got two Gold Glovers in Betts and Bradley, and Benny was in the running for one in 2018 as well, so that speaks volumes. Jimmie, Dewey, and I played really well as a unit. We moved like we were playing zone defense in football. We moved as a unit—1, 2, and 3. We all knew where each other was going to be, we all knew the responsibilities, and that's why we never ran into each other. We never fouled up, and I'm assuming these guys have that same kind of communication.

It's a little bit different from when we played because there were no analytics involved back then. Basically, I was in charge of positioning the guys because I had the best view. Say we're playing against Wade Boggs and I'm going to play in left-center and move

Jimmie toward the line, I've got to bring Dwight over with me. If I move 20 feet, I've got to move Dwight 20 feet in order to cover that gap. So basically, we're daring him to hit the ball down the right-field line, which he doesn't want to do. So, you try to position yourself where he's going to hit the ball and if he stings one, we're going to get it. Try to make him do something he doesn't want to do.

That's what's happening with the shift today. Guys don't want to hit against the shift and they keep hitting balls hard, right to where the defensive guys are. As a center fielder, it was my job to figure out what was going on. A lot of times, we'd just play straightaway but if not, if I got to right-center, I pull Jimmie over with me and if I'm going to left-center, I pull Dwight with me. But we'd always talk about those things. Or I'd just whistle and they'd move. We just didn't leave those gaping holes somewhere like major-league teams do now. Today, the analytics say the guy's not going to hit it there. Well, my analytics are my eyes and sometimes I can see that the hitter's locked in and my pitcher doesn't have it that day. How do you figure all that out using a chart? There is some space for me with those kinds of numbers and I would look at them, but they'd never be etched in stone for me. And I doubt if they are for the B's either. There's so much information that these guys are given, I don't know how much of that they're using. Are they using their own senses? I think it's probably a combination. You don't become a Gold Glove-caliber outfielder just by using what clubs are giving you out of a book. That's just not how it works.

I think these guys are pretty heady and I think they watch what the heck is going on. They'd have to because some of the plays they make—like Benny on that little sinking liner in Houston, he got a great jump on it and he *committed* to it. If he misses it, game's over. If he catches it, game's over. That's the kind of commitment you want. They're not afraid to take chances. It's educated guessing, and they all get such a good jump. But when I see that kind of stuff, I know that it's already been thought out. The ball's hit—you go! You've got to assume the ball's being hit to you *on every pitch* and that's how you make those kinds of plays. Because if you don't, you're a glove behind and the ball bounces and goes by you and two runs score and the game's over.

When I explain outfield defense to people, I call it a *want-to* position. You have to want to do it because it requires a lot of mental energy, especially the way I did it. So I'm in center and I'm literally moving. My feet are moving on every pitch. I already see where Pudge [catcher Carlton Fisk] is setting up and if he's setting up inside and the guy throws it there, I'm already moving that way. So now the ball's hit and I'm gone and again it's my footwork. I don't cross over. My feet open up because of those things I just described. I open up and I'm off. A lot of times before the guy has made his full swing, I'm already gone, anticipating where it's going to go. In center you can see where the ball's being pitched and you can lean that way, so I'm moving *on every pitch*. That takes energy, a lot of energy. I see guys today and when the pitch is thrown they're just static, they're not moving. See, that's too long to wait. You're not going to get the jump. When you play center, you've got tons of ground to cover so, as I say, that's the want-to part.

When you play in the outfield together you form a bond. You pull for one another. A few years ago at the Red Sox Winter Weekend, we had a little symposium: the Killer B's vs Jimmie, Dewey, and me. People were asking all kinds of questions, but I pulled Benny, Mookie, and Jackie off to the side to talk. I just wanted to see where they were coming from and I don't talk to many outfielders that think like me, about the "want-to" part of being an outfielder—but these guys did. I said, "OK, that's pretty cool. That's really refreshing to hear." These guys want to play defense and it shows. It really does.

I've always been a big proponent of the "defense wins championships" philosophy. Sure, you have to hit and you have to score runs, but you don't have to score as many if you don't give up as many. These guys can all throw well, too, just like my three guys. Like us, they seldom miss the cutoff guys or throw to the wrong base and we all had something on it because we could all throw. I think we have that edge on them as a group as far as arm strength goes, but there's nothing they can't do defensively. As a group, the only edge I'm giving them is speed. That's it—but that's a big one. If I was in spring training with them, I'd needle them about that too. I'd say, "If I had your speed, I'd catch every ball. The ball would never hit the ground." You just never want to let them feel they're doing everything perfectly.

If you're going to compare these guys fairly with us, they're still lacking in hitting. That's where we have them so far. Hitting for average and for power. It's still early in their careers, but Jimmie, Dwight, and I displayed those attributes very quickly. I hope it's going to happen for them soon. Obviously, Mookie has had phenomenal back-to-back seasons at the plate. He's a disciplined guy and he's unique among today's hitters in the way he approaches hitting. We always used to say: "Do what you do that got you here." Don't change unless there's a crisis. Going into the 2019 season, Jackie has decided to make a significant swing change and an adjustment in his approach at the plate. Sometimes it's a mental thing. These guys have all the physical tools, but the really good hitters are mentally higher up. They've figured things out and they just keep on going. Jackie has decided he needs an adjustment and that's part of the process. Benintendi has also experienced some highs and lows offensively. When you go through the tough times, your guard goes up and you get a little tougher mentally and it's not a bad thing sometimes, believe it or not. The important thing is that these guys have done it as a group.

Potentially, these guys could do some damage offensively, there's no question about it—and they've all hit well when it counted, in the postseason. They've already won the World Series, which we never did, so that's a big plus for their side.

My biggest hope is that these three guys will be able to stay together as a group. That would be fun to watch. I know most fans would love to see that happen. The thing that I hear most from Red Sox fans is that they were sorry I wasn't able to stay in Boston with the other guys. Well, I feel the same way. You get spoiled playing with good players; believe me, it's true. Sometimes you go somewhere else and the players aren't as good and you go, *OK, I have to adjust.* And then your role expands and you do more than you were doing before. You were doing a lot before but now you're doing even more and all of a sudden people are saying, "Gee, he looks like he's slowed down." Nope, didn't slow down; just covering more ground.

In an ideal world it would be nice to keep this group intact: Benintendi, Bradley, and Betts. They're still young guys but I'm sure they know how fortunate they are to be part of this special team. For the next generation of Red Sox fans, this is the only outfield they will look back at with nostalgia. Just as we were for a previous generation. It would be great to be able to watch them as they progress. If you asked them, I think they'd say the same thing. In any case, enjoy them, because outfields like this don't come around too often.

—Fred Lynn, Carlsbad, California,
February 14, 2019

Photo by Natalie Lynn

Introduction

Seldom has being a Red Sox fan felt so good. The dark days are gone. Where pessimism was once rampant, optimism abounds. Cynicism is on the run. The Fellowship of the Miserable has been disbanded, or at least repurposed. Since its 86-year-old championship drought ended in 2004, the team has taken us on a roller coaster ride of highs and lows during which we've now won four World Series in this young century. Fans old enough to remember back a few decades, before Papi and Schilling and Epstein, are ecstatic. Many thought they'd never see this reversal of fortune. Truth be told, that 2004 title was so sweet that it might have sustained many of us for another 86 years. Younger fans, accustomed to winning, now expect more. The good news is that they have a good chance to have those expectations met.

The current Red Sox lineup is loaded with youthful talent at virtually every position, and nowhere is that truer than in the outfield.

The Boston Red Sox have been blessed with a lot of great outfielders over the years. Tris Speaker played center field like none before or since. Left fielder Ted Williams was probably the best hitter in the history of the game. Harry Hooper was a superb right fielder and remains the only Red Sox player to win four World Series rings with the team.

Fred Lynn, Jim Rice, Reggie Smith, Jim Piersall, Dewey Evans, Tony Conigliaro. The list goes on and on and we can all put together our own personal all-time outfield if we cherry-pick from different teams and different eras. But what about the greatest Red Sox outfield that ever played together at the same time? Or the greatest outfield in the game today?

Choosing the best Red Sox outfield of all time is challenging for a number of reasons. For one thing, it's always difficult to assess players from the early part of the last century. Oh sure, there's a lot of anecdotal evidence and some impressive statistics, but without actually seeing them in action, we are limited in what we know. The other challenge in selecting an all-time outfield is choosing players who are outstanding both offensively and defensively.

Williams was arguably the best-hitting player of all time, but does he deserve to be mentioned among the best left fielders when you factor in his glove work? Carl Yastrzemski was a fantastic hitter and a great fielder. He knew how to play balls hit off the wall and did all the little things that add up to big things. You have to strike a balance and determine what having a Gold Glove outfielder really means to a team. Or what having a .300 hitter with 25 homers means if his defense is mediocre. Good field, no hit. Good hit, no field. The old-timers used to say that for certain positions it didn't really matter what you batted if your defense was solid. Catchers often fit into that category and so did the second basemen and shortstops, the essential "strength up the middle" guys. In the 1970s, shortstop Mark Belanger of the Baltimore Orioles regularly batted in the low .220s and never exceeded five homers in a season—but he won eight Gold Gloves and was considered a star. Even today, catchers who know how to call a game, have great defensive skills, and showcase a strong arm to second can bat .250 and enjoy a successful major-league career.

Expectations for outfielders are much higher. Like quarterbacks in football and power forwards in basketball, they are the glamour boys of baseball. The Willie Mayses, Hank Aarons,

Mickey Mantles, Duke Sniders, and Joe DiMaggios are expected to do it all, both at the plate and in the field.

So which was the greatest Red Sox outfield unit of all time? The cover of the April 11, 1970 issue of *The Sporting News* features a beautiful cover shot of Yaz, Reggie Smith, and Tony Conigliaro, accompanied by the caption, "Is This Baseball's Greatest Outfield?" Perhaps at that exact moment in time they were the best. It's especially tough for fans to be objective. When the Red Sox broke the 86-year curse in 2004, the outfield consisted of Manny Ramirez in left, Johnny Damon in center, and either Gabe Kapler or Trot Nixon in right. Manny batted .308 with 43 homers and 130 RBIs but played left field like he was trying to find his way out of a corn maze. Damon batted .304 with 20 homers and 94 RBIs, but the bearded caveman's arm was so weak that when he later left to join the Yankees, Sox fans claimed that he "looks like Jesus, acts like Judas, and throws like Mary." Kapler and Nixon both did capable jobs in right field but would never be mistaken for Dewey Evans. But for brand-new fans and many of those who suffered through the long World Series drought, they are an outfield to remember.

The point is that there are lots of very good outfields but only a handful that should be under consideration as the best ever. Generations ago, Sox historians marveled at what they dubbed the "Golden Outfield."

The Golden Outfield

For six magical seasons, from 1910 to 1915, the then-powerhouse Boston Red Sox featured a fielding trio known as the "Golden Outfield," namely Duffy Lewis in left, Tris Speaker in center, and Harry Hooper in right.

They were easily the best defensive combination of the day, featuring superior speed and great instincts. They also had powerful arms and reflexes usually associated with infielders.

His great speed allowed Tris Speaker to play the shallowest center field in the history of the game. He was like an extra infielder as evidenced by the fact that he took part in 64 double plays during his nine-year stay in Boston. Speaker had a record number of outfield assists. He was no slouch at the plate, either, batting .337 for the Sox. In 1912 he captured the American League MVP award.

Harry Hooper was so good in right field that the league changed a rule because of him. Hooper employed a gimmick whereby he'd juggle a caught ball while running to the infield. This froze any runners trying to advance until the ball settled in his glove. The new rule allowed runners to advance the moment the ball hit the glove. Hooper batted a modest .272 with the Red Sox, but the number of runs he prevented from scoring made him invaluable.

Duffy Lewis batted .286 while with Boston and is one of a handful of Red Sox players to have had a Fenway Park landmark named for him. At the time, Fenway's left field ground was graded to slant dramatically upward toward the wall. Lewis was a master at playing this unique slope and it was soon dubbed Duffy's Cliff. It would be interesting to speculate how Andrew Benintendi, Ted Williams, Jim Rice, or even Carl Yastrzemski would have handled the cliff.

Speaker and Hooper are enshrined in the Baseball Hall of Fame in Cooperstown. Babe Ruth and Ty Cobb both called the three the greatest outfield of all time—and that certainly speaks volumes. But perhaps the biggest argument for the supremacy of this outfield is the fact that the Red Sox won two World Series during their tenure (1912, 1915). And even after Speaker was traded just before the 1916 season, they won another. With Lewis in the Navy, Hooper was part of a fourth World Series-winning Red Sox team—the only player in Red Sox history to win four world championships with the team.

Interestingly, one thing this outfield did not have was camaraderie. Lewis hated Speaker and Speaker hated Lewis. Despite this mutual loathing, they not only did their jobs but excelled at them.

The new gold standard for Red Sox outfields would have to be the trio of Jim Rice in left, Fred Lynn in center, and Dewey Evans in right. How talented were they? They were so talented that they once played together for three innings in an All-Star Game. Two of them—Lynn and Evans—were Gold Glovers and all three became skilled in handling the special challenges of Fenway Park.

Jim Rice was such a great hitter that his fielding was over-looked, but he made himself into a competent glove man. And all three could hit for power and for average. In fact, their status as Boston's greatest all-time outfield has remained pretty much unchallenged since they parted company. Watching Evans going back to the right-field wall and then throwing behind a runner sent chills through a generation of Red Sox fans. And was there ever a more graceful center fielder than Lynn? Who can forget his valiant effort, slamming into the unforgiving Fenway wall in Game Six of the 1975 World Series? And Rice played balls off the Monster with expertise, cutting down an army of runners at second. The case for best Red Sox outfield seemed closed.

Then, some 40 years later, Andrew Benintendi, Mookie Betts, and Jackie Bradley Jr. joined forces, and old arguments were replaced by exciting new conjecture. Several more seasons of playing together will have to enter the record books before they can challenge for the title of best Red Sox outfield, and there are many things that could derail their claim: injury, extended hitting woes, and baseball economics, for example. But the very fact that these three have entered the discussion is significant.

Perhaps the fairer question would be: what is Major League Baseball's best outfield *today*? Again, you have to consider offense and defense, but the comparisons are somewhat more quantifiable. In an October 18, 2018 article in *FanGraphs*, writer Jeff Sullivan reported the results of their statistical analysis.[1] The comparison covers the past 17 seasons and is based on the greatest single season.

Top Major League Outfields, 2002—2018

Team	Year	Batting Runs	Base-running Runs	Fielding Runs	WAR
Red Sox	2018	100.0	14.6	26.4	20.5
Braves	2004	73.1	6.9	51.1	18.5
Giants	2002	93.5	13.7	20.1	18.5
Angels	2012	63.9	19.6	24.7	17.2
Braves	2002	97.5	1.6	14.6	17.0
Blue Jays	2006	72.1	4.3	34.1	16.8
Brewers	2018	63.9	14.1	27.6	16.7
Yankees	2011	55.7	11.9	33.0	16.5
Cardinals	2002	80.8	7.4	20.5	16.5
Marlins	2017	99.6	-0.9	8.8	16.5

For those who embrace such metrics, that should be enough. But for many seeing is believing and, if anything, seeing only strengthens the case for the Betts/Bradley/Benintendi outfield. All three made heart-stopping catches in 2018. They also made game-saving catches, home-run-robbing catches, off-the-wall catches, and a variety of other hyphenated-type catches.

For those of us whose love of baseball extends back well beyond this 17-season assessment, the author, Jeff Sullivan, offers the following list of great offensive outfields:

Top Hitting Outfields

Team	Year	sOPS+
Yankees	1927	148
Yankees	1941	144
Indians	1994	144
Red Sox	1979	141
Yankees	1939	140
Yankees	1928	139

Yankees	1940	139
Cardinals	1948	138
Rockies	1997	138
Red Sox	2018	138

SOURCE: Baseball-Reference.com's OPS+ compares the team split to the league-average split.

As one can see, the 2018 Red Sox outfielders are in an eighth-place tie with the 1997 Colorado Rockies as the best hitting outfield in history over a single season. Factor in their speed, their base-running skills, their baseball smarts, and their unselfish play and perhaps they advance a few notches.

The premise of this book is that Benintendi, Bradley, and Betts are the best overall outfield in baseball today. But it's more than that. We also tell the story of each of these talented young athletes. There are two things that happened as we began to research and write. Our respect for each of them, already high, increased. The other thing that came to light was the fact that this outfield is not just Benintendi and Bradley and Betts; it's the unit—the Benintendi-Bradley-Betts outfield, or as we like to call it, The Killer B's (we added an honorary fourth Killer B in the person of Brock Holt because on any given day he can fill in for any of them and the Red Sox don't miss an offensive or defensive beat). These outstanding players have very different backgrounds and come from different socioeconomic circumstances, but you don't have to look far to see the commonalities that dwarf these superficial differences. They all had incredible support from their parents. They all earned their way to the majors and did so in very short order. Once there, they didn't rest on their laurels, and they continue to work hard to improve all aspects of their game.

The Killer B's are fun to watch. They go all-out all the time. They enjoy the game. They honor the game. They play the game the way it should be played, with respect for each other and for opposing players. They have the full attention of fans across the major leagues, including Jim Rice, Fred Lynn, and Dwight Evans, the new gold standard against which they will inevitably be measured.

Andrew Benintendi, Left Field

In New England, virtually every promising pro athlete is measured by the yardstick of past legends. For Celtics players that means comparisons with Bill Russell or Larry Bird. For the Patriots, the gold standard has been set by quarterback Tom Brady. For the Bruins, it starts and stops with Number 4, Bobby Orr. Since their founding in 1901, the Boston Red Sox have had many legendary players, at least one at every position. But nowhere in Boston sports has a higher bar been established for greatness than in Fenway's left field, current domain of Andrew Benintendi.

Little wonder that Benintendi is cursed with great expectations. It's a natural consequence of having your swing compared to left fielder Ted Williams and your glove work to left fielder Carl Yastrzemski. Reminders of Number 9 and Number 8 can be found everywhere at Fenway Park. Their retired numbers are hung high on the façade beyond right field for all to see. The seat where Ted blasted a 502-foot home run is the only one painted red in a sea of green. There are statues and pictures and a thousand other tributes inside and outside the park and the souvenir shops are well stocked with Yaz and Ted merchandise. The biggest reminder of their Hall of Fame careers is left field itself. It's the closest thing to hallowed ground in the venerable old ballpark.

With notable pauses for World War II and Korea, Ted Williams trod on it from 1940 to 1960 (he played right field his rookie year of 1939), although he was often more focused on his next at-bat than the next line drive hit his way. When Ted finally hung 'em up after a homer in his last at-bat, in stepped Carl Yastrzemski, a potato farmer's son from Long Island, New York.

Yastrzemski, Fenway's legendary Lord of Left Field, is high on today's youthful Red Sox outfield. In a 2019 spring training interview with Chad Jennings of *The Athletic*, the 79-year-old Hall of Famer calls them "the best in the American League and maybe in both leagues."[2] Like his former teammate Lynn, he bases his assessment on his own two eyes, not the new analytics that have supposedly rendered expert opinions like his outdated, if not downright quaint.

There are some fascinating connections between Yaz and the current Sox outfielders. In the Impossible Dream season of 1967, Yaz almost single-handedly led the Red Sox to the World Series, winning the Triple Crown in the process. His Wins Above Replacement (WAR) that season (undoubtedly a metric that he knows little about) was the highest in Red Sox history and third highest in major-league history by a position player. Mookie Betts's WAR in his 2018 MVP campaign was second highest in Red Sox history. And when the current occupant of left field, Andrew Benintendi, took his position in left field on Opening Day in 2017, he was the youngest ever to do so—except for Yastrzemski, who was 40 days younger when he did so in the 1961 opener.

Benintendi knows the responsibility that comes with being heir to this special part of Fenway. "There's obviously been a lot of great players who played left field [at Fenway Park]," he told Jennings. "Just kind of being around Boston for a little bit now, I kind of learn more about it every year."

Meanwhile, Captain Carl watches every Red Sox game on TV and he loves what he sees. "The Red Sox are very lucky to have these three outfielders. They're young. They can run. And, like I said, they can play defense, and they're tremendous on the offensive part of the field."

Yaz possesses insights that only the Lord of Left can have. The one sight he refuses to use is hindsight. Asked to compare his own accomplishments to those of the Killer B's, he says, "I never think about it. Different eras, completely."[3]

Yaz ended up playing more games than anyone else in Red Sox history. He was *the* Red Sox star for a generation of fans. Yaz was the primary guardian of the Green Monster from 1961 to 1974, after which Jim Rice took charge from 1975 to 1989. As with Ted, it was Rice's hitting, not fielding, that propelled the Boston Strongman to the Hall of Fame. Thus, for almost a half-century, left field was the domain of three consecutive Hall of Famers.

Mike Greenwell and Troy O'Leary performed in the shadow of the Green Monster—and in the shadows of their predecessors—until Manny Ramirez brought his own style to the unique piece of real estate from 2001 to 2008. Since then there's been a parade of pretenders to Fenway's left-field fiefdom, but fans have patiently awaited the arrival of a true and rightful heir. It was up to Benny to pull that sword from a stone. Hence the expectations, the price tag of promise.

Red Sox fans are among the most knowledgeable and loyal in baseball. They idolize past heroes, and newcomers must prove themselves. They also appreciate talent and they revere blue-collar effort. Benintendi offers both, which bodes well for the future.

Former Red Sox center fielder Fred Lynn is uniquely positioned to offer informed commentary on some legendary Fenway left fielders. From 1974 to 1980, he played alongside Jim Rice and saw Yaz play the position before he moved to first base. These days he watches Benintendi and his outfield mates from the comfort of his home in Carlsbad, California. Their exploits bring back a flood of memories. They also invite comparisons.

"Rice had good straight-ahead speed," Lynn says. "He wasn't shifty or anything like that, but he ran pretty well. In 1978 [his MVP season], he had fifteen triples, so he could move. In terms of arm strength, I think he probably throws a little bit better than Benny. Benny's probably a better all-around outfielder because he could play center if needed, but if we're just talking defense, it's pretty close. Benny's probably got a little bit more quickness.

"In terms of playing in left field and playing the wall, things are different now. The wall itself is different. When Jimmie and I came up it was concrete and then tin, a different composition than it is these days. I don't know what it's made of, but it's not wood; it's some kind of fabricated substance where the ball comes off pretty evenly. Back in the day Jim would assume the ball was going to hit the tin Monster and fall straight down. He would grab it in the air and peg it to second, either throwing the guy out or keeping him from going to second. He was really good at it, and Yaz was also very good at it too. My job was always to back Jimmie up in case it hit one of the studs and ricocheted out. Of course, Yaz was so good he could grab those as well."

Although it has remained fundamentally unchanged over its long history, Fenway has undergone a number of subtle alterations since Lynn and company played there. Even left field has been impacted. "The scoreboard goes almost from center to the line so when they put the numbers up, the ball is going to carom off them and it's going to be haphazard. When it hits the scoreboard, it comes straight down unless it hits at an odd angle, so Benny should have a pretty good advantage because when Jimmie played the ball could ricochet 20 feet. It's probably a little easier to play now, but it still has the doorway down the left-field line and there are still lots of things you still need to know.

"Jimmie learned how to decoy from Carl [Yastrzemski] and no, Carl did *not* learn it from Ted [Williams]! Ted was a good hitter—a great hitter—and we'll leave it at that. But Carl was really good at playing left. He really knew that wall and played it better than anybody as far as I could see. Now I didn't play left field that much when I was there because Jimmie had to play there—and by then Yaz was at first. Jimmie could really decoy them. I mean you have time. You read the ball off the bat and you don't know where it's going to go—off the wall—you can make like you're going to catch it or if it's going to be in the net, you just look up and get it off the wall real quickly and get it in to second base. Benny and Jimmie both do that pretty well."

Andrew Benintendi was born in Cincinnati, Ohio, on July 6, 1994, to Jill and Chris Benintendi. Chris is an attorney and it was left to Jill to take care of raising Andrew and his two sisters, Olivia and Lily. The sporting gene was dominant in both parents. Jill Brookbank Benintendi is honored in the Ripley High School Hall of Fame for scoring a total of 1,246 points for the Lady Jays basketball team. Jill's father, Donald Brookbank (Andrew's grandfather), was a 2009 Hall of Fame inductee at Higginsport High School in basketball, baseball, and track. His aunt Kelly Benintendi had scored 2,366 points for Georgetown High basketball teams. Meanwhile, father Chris played third base at Georgetown High and at Division III Wittenberg University. This was one athletic family.

Benintendi attended Madeira High School, about 25 miles northeast of Cincinnati. He played high school ball for the Madeira High Mustangs and hit .564 as a senior, with a dozen home runs, 57 RBIs, 63 runs scored, and 38 stolen bases. He achieved national recognition when the American Baseball Coaches Association named him National High School Player of the Year. Like his outfield mate, 5-foot-9 Mookie Betts, the 5-foot-10 Benintendi also starred at high school basketball, averaging 25.5 points per game, and was the 2011–12 *Cincinnati Enquirer*'s Division III Co-Player of the Year.

Andrew's dad grew up a diehard fan of the Big Red Machine Cincinnati teams of the 1970s. In the 2013 major-league draft, the hometown Reds selected his son, but not until the 31st round, as overall selection No. 945. Despite a sentimental connection, the younger Benintendi elected not to sign and enrolled instead at the University of Arkansas. As a freshman he played in 61 games, all but one in the outfield. Batting at or near the top of the lineup, he hit .276 with eight doubles, 27 runs batted in, and 45 runs scored. He also showed some speed on the basepaths, swiping 17 bases and earning a spot on the SEC All-Freshman Team.

His sophomore year was nothing short of spectacular. He led the SEC in hitting with a .376 average and the country in homers with 20. He stole 20 bases and led the league in slugging percentage (.717), on-base percentage (.488), and bases on balls (50). He finished third in the country in slugging percentage at .736 and hit .443 in 29 SEC games, with a .527 on-base percentage. At one point he reached base safely in 26 consecutive games, including 41 of his last 59 plate appearances. He was named the 2015 Southeastern Conference Player of the Year, the first Razorback so honored, during a College World Series-bound season for Arkansas.

Statue

Andrew Benintendi hadn't played a single inning of major-league baseball and already he had more hardware than Home Depot. He had won the Golden Spikes Award, the Dick Howser Trophy, the SEC Male Athlete of the Year award, *Baseball America* National Player of the Year Award, Collegiate Baseball National Player of the Year, and SEC Coaches' Player of the Year.

He was an All-SEC First Team selection, a Louisville Slugger All-America First Team selection, an ABCA/Rawlings All-America First Team selection, an NCBWA All-America First Team selection, a D1Baseball All-America First Team member, and a *Baseball America* All-America First Team selection. And that's just a partial list.

But while trophies and plaques are all well and good, they tend to be kept indoors to be enjoyed by an exclusive group of friends and family. Fans of the Arkansas Razorbacks felt he deserved something bigger, something grander, something that would allow easier accessibility to people and, presumably, pigeons. That's right, they felt that Benny deserved a statue.

Longtime sportswriter and editor Steve Andrews, who covered the Razorbacks early in his career and has worked for major newspapers in North Carolina and Florida, started it all. He's such a fan that even Benny, his cat, was named after him. "He's the only player in any of the major sports to ever be named unanimous national player of the year," says Andrews. "Coupled with his humble personality and fan friendliness, I decided to start a movement to get a statue of him at Baum Stadium, home of the Razorbacks. I think it's very much deserved."[4]

Usually statues, if they come at all, come only after a long and brilliant career. Even Ted Williams didn't get one until long after he retired, although he now has several, including two outside Fenway Park and one at the Baseball Hall of Fame in Cooperstown. Yaz also has one at Fenway. And then there's The Teammates statue outside Fenway's Gate B, a moving tribute in bronze to Williams, Dom DiMaggio, Johnny Pesky, and Bobby Doerr.

It may be a tad premature, but perhaps someday there'll be another cluster of statues at Fenway called The Killer B's, featuring Benintendi, Bradley, Betts, and Brock Holt.

His decision to attend Arkansas had been a good one, but after his sophomore year he made the decision to turn pro. One benefit of the Red Sox finishing in last place in 2014 was that it gave them a high draft pick. Selected seventh overall in the June 8, 2015 draft, Andrew Benintendi was the earliest-ever college player selected by the Sox in a June draft. He received a signing bonus reported at $3.6 million. Waiting to sign had paid off in more ways than one.

More awards followed in rapid succession, including three prestigious national honors. On June 11, he was presented with the *Baseball America* National Player of the Year Award. The very next day, he won the Dick Howser Trophy as the best college player in the country. And on June 23, 2015, Benintendi captured the coveted Golden Spikes Award as the best amateur player in the country. (Other Red Sox players to win the prestigious award include Jason Varitek, David Price, and J. D. Drew. Benintendi was the seventh outfielder to capture the honor; the first was Terry Francona in 1980.) He had a little difficulty dealing with all the attention, said Razorbacks coach Dave van Horn. "It's been a humbling time," Benintendi himself admitted. "I've had a lot of help to get where I am. I'm not doing this just for me but for everybody who has gotten me to where I am. I'm trying to soak it all in."[5]

The ink was still drying on the contractual paperwork when the Boston Red Sox put Benintendi to work in their minor-league system. He was on the fast track to the majors, moving through his stops so quickly he made speed dates look like long-term commitments. In little more than a year he'd be in the majors.

On July 3, he started in center field for the Lowell Spinners of the Class-A short-season New York–Penn League. He appeared in 35 games by August 16, when he was moved to the Class-A Greenville Drive in South Carolina. In the 35 games he played for Lowell, he was error-free in the field and hit .290 (.408 on-base percentage) with seven homers and 15 RBIs. He stole seven bases. For Greenville, he upped his average to .351 (.430 OBP) over 19 games, with an OPS (on-base plus slugging) of 1.011.

He had trained with the Red Sox in 2016 and was 2-for-3 with a run scored in his first spring-training game on March 18, 2016.

Back in Boston, Benintendi was now an unmistakable and fast-approaching blip on the Red Sox radar. Promoted to the Salem Red Sox in 2016, he picked up where he'd left off the previous season, thriving under the intense scrutiny of team scouts. From April 7 to May 15, he appeared in 34 Carolina League games and drove in 32 runs while batting .341.

Yet another promotion was in order, this time to the Double-A Portland Sea Dogs. In 63 games, through the end of July, he drove in 44 runs with eight homers and batted .295. Up to this juncture, Benintendi had played almost exclusively in center field. The Red Sox already had one of the best center fielders in the game in Jackie Bradley Jr., so in late July the parent team asked that he be moved to left field at Portland's Hadlock Field. It was a position he had never played before, but the request was consistent with the Red

Sox's big-picture strategy. After he had come up to the big leagues, he explained what that thinking had been: "They try to teach us to play all three [outfield] positions. Center field's where I played in college and last year, but I think that being able to play left has helped me."[6]

Hadlock has its own version of the Green Monster and on July 22, Benintendi got to experience it for the first time. The learning curve would be steep but he faced the challenge head-on, and his only minor-league error in all of 2016 (242 chances) came while playing center field in Salem. Four of his final nine starts in the minors were in left field.

The Boston brain trust had seen enough. Portland was to be his last minor-league outpost. He had climbed the minor-league ladder two rungs at a time and skipped the top rung altogether. On August 1, he was called up to the Red Sox, so fast that he scarcely had time to master the Maine accent before he was asked to tackle the one in Beantown. He soon found out that being called a "wicked pissah" is a good thing.

He was destined to make his first major-league appearance less than 14 months after being drafted. Like Jackie Bradley Jr., he entered the major-league fraternity without ever having played a game at Triple A.

Benintendi's major-league debut came on August 2, 2016, in Seattle. The Red Sox were leading the Mariners, 3–0, in the top of the seventh. With two outs, manager John Farrell looked down the bench and asked Andrew to pinch-hit for left fielder Bryce Brentz. Benny grounded out to second base in his first major-league at-bat. Benintendi then took the field in left and played there the final three innings of the game. He never had a ball hit to him, but he did watch one soar over his head. The Sox added one run in the top of the eighth on a solo home run by David Ortiz, but David Price lost his shutout—and more—in the bottom of the eighth. The first batter up, Mike Zunino, homered to left-center. Before the inning was over, the Mariners scored five times to take the lead. With two outs in the top of the ninth, and reliever Edwin Diaz on the mound, Benintendi struck out looking on three pitches. For Benintendi, it was a less than dramatic entrance onto the big-league stage, but there was always the next day. Meanwhile, his father had missed seeing his son's introduction to the majors; he'd fallen asleep in front of the TV in the fifth inning.

The following day Chris Benintendi was in Seattle, in person and fully awake, to see his son play his second major-league game. The Mariners emerged victorious once again, but Benintendi got the start in left field and played his first full game. Batting ninth in the order, he came up in the third inning and hit a clean line drive to left field for a single off Hisashi Iwakuma. It was his first major-league base hit. He struck out his next time up, but in the top of the eighth made it a 2-for-3 day, singling to right field. He was on his way.

On August 7, at Dodger Stadium, he collected his first runs batted in—two of them. He singled to left-center in the third and stole his first base. With runners on first and second in the top of the fourth, he hit a two-out single to right field to drive in Brock Holt. In the top of the sixth, he came up again with two outs, this time with Aaron Hill on second base. He singled to right field again, driving in Hill. And he crossed the plate himself with his first big-league run two batters later, when Mookie Betts singled him in. He'd had a 3-for-4 day in front of his original hitting coach and biggest fan, his dad.

It's one thing to open on the road but quite another to perform in front of the hometown crowd. The next game was at Fenway Park in Boston on August 9, against the New York Yankees. Benny was about to experience firsthand the intense spotlight of the biggest rivalry in sports. It didn't take long for him to endear himself to the Fenway faithful. Benny brought the crowd to its feet with his first extra-base hit, a fifth-inning RBI double off Luis Severino. The knock earned him a subhead in the next morning's *Boston Globe*:

"Rookie Benintendi leads rally that topples Yankees." There are few things that please the Boston populace more than tearing a strip off the Pinstripes.

Never mind that the two-bagger had actually been a bit of a disappointment at the time. Sandy Leon had tripled to lead off the inning. Benintendi then hit a ball to deep left-center that struck the wall near the yellow line. To the right of the line it would have been a home run, but the umpire ruled it was still in play—thus, a double. Red Sox manager John Farrell came out and argued. The umpires convened and changed their ruling to a home run. But then Yankees manager Joe Girardi called for a review and the Replay Operations Center in New York reversed the call yet again, ruling that it was a double. Benny was getting a crash course on the geopolitical nature of Fenway, where nothing is clear-cut and disputes over boundaries are commonplace. Despite the bizarre double-to-homer-to double call, the Red Sox won the game, the first full game in which Benny had appeared that resulted in victory.

It hadn't taken long for the handsome young man from the Midwest to win over the citizenry of Red Sox Nation. On August 9, 2016, sports columnist, author, and passionate Red Sox fan Bill Simmons tweeted the following: "Benintendi rapidly climbing the ladder of most important people in my life . . . I think he just passed 10 cousins, 4 uncles and 3 aunts."

His first game-winning hit was recorded on August 14. It came off Zach Greinke of the Arizona Diamondbacks and drove in the third run in a 16–2 win. A week later, on August 21 in Detroit, Benintendi finally got his first permanent, irreversible home run. It was a two-run shot off Shane Greene in the top of the seventh, cutting the Tigers' lead to 10–5, but the Red Sox still lost.

During his early days in Boston, it often seemed that Benintendi's hair garnered as much attention as his on-field exploits. It had remained unshorn since his stay in Portland and now that he was in the majors, he didn't want to tempt fate by visiting a barber shop. His coif became so large that he was actually in the market for a larger hat until his mom paid a visit. Suddenly he decided a haircut was in order, proving that even the awesome power of player superstition takes a back seat to the power of parental supervision.

A baserunning mishap caused him to miss 20 games from August 25 to September 15. He went on the DL due to a left knee sprain, but was fitted for a custom knee brace, returned, and finished up nicely.

His best game of the year was probably the September 21 contest in Baltimore. The Red Sox won, 5–1, and Benny drove in three of the five runs with one mighty blow, first-pitch swinging and homering over the right-field scoreboard.

By season's end, Andrew had the same .295 batting average he'd recorded at Portland, with an on-base percentage of .359, marginally higher than the .357 he had recorded with the Sea Dogs. He had driven in 14 runs and scored 16 in 34 games, collecting 31 hits, two of them homers. In the field, he handled 56 chances with only one error.

Based on his regular-season showing, the Red Sox decided to add the newcomer to the playoff roster. In his first postseason plate appearance in the ALDS opener, Benintendi homered at Cleveland's Progressive Field off the Indians' Trevor Bauer. Cleveland swept the Division Series from the Red Sox in three games but of the seven runs the Sox managed to score, two were driven in by Benintendi. The 22-year-old's homer made him the youngest Red Sox player to go deep in a postseason contest. "There's a lot at stake in these games," he told the *Boston Globe*'s Peter Abraham, "but it's still baseball. I try and remind myself of that."[7] Sox manager John Farrell was impressed with his performance under pressure. "He's extremely poised," he said. "For a guy that 16 months ago, he was on the University of Arkansas campus, it's pretty remarkable. He's been a guy that's never really panicked, even when he's been in a pretty disadvantaged count at the plate. His athletic movements are graceful. It's almost like a window into what his mind is going through. It's even, it's under control, and he plays like that."[8]

In December 2016, the recently-retired David Ortiz pointed to all three outfielders—and Xander Bogaerts—as players the Red Sox should lock up with long-term contracts. Impressed with their skill and work ethic, he said, "Those are the players you want on your ballclub. Young and talented, with that mentality."[9]

He'd appeared in only 34 games with 105 at-bats in 2016, well short of the 45 games or 130 at-bats needed to qualify as a rookie. This meant that 2017 would be Benintendi's official rookie season. He went to spring training ranked by *Baseball America* as the No. 1 prospect in the game.

The Red Sox wanted to acquire pitcher Chris Sale from the White Sox, and some observers were concerned that Benintendi might be sacrificed as trade bait. Instead, the Red Sox let another top prospect, Yoan Moncada, go and wisely held onto Benintendi. For his part Benny said he was glad that he wouldn't have to bat against Sale. Dave Dombrowski, President of Baseball Operations for the Red Sox, later claimed that they were never close to trading Benintendi.[10]

Between workouts at 2017 spring training in Fort Myers, Benintendi told Peter Abraham that he planned to work on his defense most of all—to try to bring it up to something approaching the level of JBJ in center and Mookie Betts in right. "It's a benefit to me, being a part of a group like that . . . I think we can have one of the best defensive outfields in the game."[11] Then-outfield coach Ruben Amaro Jr. worked with him to adjust his mechanics to the different requirements of throwing from left rather than center field.

It would prove to be a remarkable outfield in many ways, one of them being that all three B's—Benintendi, Bradley, and Betts—were listed at 5-foot-9 or 5-foot-10. Benintendi told the *Boston Globe*'s Dan Shaughnessy, "I'm still waiting for my growth spurt."[12] Benny had added some bulk to his frame however, adding 15 or 20 pounds of muscle over the winter months through exercise and diet. They were also among the least talkative outfield trios in recent Red Sox history, preferring to let their play speak for them.

Youngest Since Yaz (2017)

When he started on Opening Day, April 3, 2017, at Fenway, Benny became the youngest Red Sox Opening Day starter in left field since Carl Yastrzemski in 1962. Having graced the cover of *Baseball America* during the springtime, he was now anything but anonymous.

With some major-league experience under his belt, he began the new campaign with a flourish. The Opening Day opposition was the NL's Pittsburgh Pirates and Benintendi had been moved from the ninth spot in the batting order to second, between Dustin Pedroia and Mookie Betts. He responded with a three-run homer to right field off Gerrit Cole in the bottom of the fifth, an inning after JBJ had made a spectacular catch in center, running 30 years to track down a ball before he bounced roughly off the wall.

On April 9, Bradley suffered a sprained right knee ligament and Benintendi moved over to center field for a dozen games. Chris Young played left, but Benintendi made sure to get in some left-field work before each game.

He remained hot at the plate, hitting over .300 until mid-May, but then settled into a .270 groove that soon deepened into a rut. He hit a point in May where he went 26 at-bats without a base hit; it was the first time in his career he'd really struggled. "This will make him a better player," said Red Sox assistant hitting coach Victor Rodriguez.[13]

His first big night at Fenway Park came on June 13 when he hit a ball into the right-field corner in the bottom of the 12th, scoring Bogaerts and winning the game. During the post-game hijinks, he was drenched with the double-barrel treatment—water and orange Gatorade. A slightly less dramatic game-winner came a month later on Flag Day. Chris Young had started in left but Benny came in during the seventh. In the bottom of the ninth, with the bases loaded, he drew a base on balls to plate the winning run, beating the Yankees at Fenway Park. He tossed his bat and jogged to first base to make it official.

His smooth swing and deft play in the outfield had attracted the attention of major-league scouts and suddenly his name was in the mix whenever trade talks were broached. Cubs manager Joe Maddon called him "Fred Lynn incarnate." There was no question that he was a legitimate contender for Rookie of the Year. As the 2017 season got underway, the late, great Nick Cafardo led off a Sunday column in the May 7 *Boston Globe*: "I've resisted the temptation to anoint Andrew Benintendi the next Fred Lynn, but I'm wavering . . . When Cubs manager Joe Maddon calls him 'Fred Lynn reincarnated,' I cringe a little because it's too early to go that far. . . . Then you watch him every day and you start thinking, could he be better than Lynn?"

On August 12, Benny had a spectacular game at Yankee Stadium, hitting two three-run homers off Luis Severino. The Sox won the game, 11–5. Among those in attendance was Andrew's paternal grandfather, Robert Benintendi, celebrating his 85th birthday. He was a Brooklyn native who had grown up a Yankees fan. "Not anymore," he said after the game.[14] Before the year was done, Benny had hit five home runs at Yankee Stadium, the most ever by a rookie on the road playing against the Yankees. It was clear by mid-August that the battle for Rookie of the Year honors was between the Yankees' highly touted phenom Aaron Judge and Boston's Benintendi.

Speaking of fives, in 2017 he had two five-hit games (April 23 in Baltimore and July 4 in Texas). That made him the first Red Sox rookie to ever manage five hits in more than one game in a season. The most he could muster in a 2018 game was four. However, even though he played three fewer games in 2018 than in 2017 (manager Alex Cora had emphasized the importance of players getting some rest at times), Benintendi hit 15 more doubles and scored 19 more runs than in the prior year. His batting and OPS both went up as well.

Overall, Benintendi saw action in 151 games and of his 155 hits, 26 were doubles and 20 were homers. He batted a respectable .271 with a .352 OBP and a slugging percentage of .424. He'd also helped the Red Sox win the AL East crown for the second year in a row. Once again they lost out in the Division Series, this time in four games to the Houston Astros, but in an encore of the previous year, he once again homered and drove in two runs in postseason play.

In many seasons it would have been enough to earn him American League Rookie of the Year honors, but 2017 also happened to be the rookie season for New York Yankee wunderkind Mr. Judge. It was a little tough to compete with Judge's league-leading 52 home runs and 128 runs scored, although it must be noted that Judge also led the league by striking out 208 times. Not surprisingly, Judge was the unanimous choice for American League Rookie of the Year, but Andrew got 23 of the 30 second-place votes. Trey Mancini of the Orioles placed third. Benny may have finished as runner-up to the undeniable Judge in the voting, but the verdict of Red Sox fans was quite the opposite. In the hometown court of public opinion, the Fenway jury liked what it saw.

Benintendi Provides Winning Margin in 15 Games (2018)

The Boston Red Sox won 108 games in 2018 to beat out a Yankees team that won 100. Of the 108 wins, Andrew Benintendi provided the game-winning hits in 15 of them. That's 14 percent, for those of you scoring at home.

His final statistics showcase a tale of two seasons. In 148 games he batted .290 with 16 homers, 41 doubles, and 21 stolen bases. Considering that the 24-year-old hit 14 of those homers in the first half of the season and only two after the All-Star break, the discrepancy left many fans shaking their heads. There are many possible reasons for the dip, but statisticians indicated that his "hard-hit" ball rate dropped significantly.

Both his bases on balls rate (10.7 percent) and strikeout rate (16 percent) remained outstanding and his ability to hit to all fields was a definite asset on a team where base runners abounded.

He may have finished second to Judge in the ROY balloting in 2017, but in 2018 he helped the Red Sox win a world championship, an honor as yet to elude the aforementioned Judge.

The Red Sox three-peated as AL East champs, this time with a very comfortable eight-game gap separating them from the second-place Yankees. Amazingly, this was a Yankees team that won 100 games, usually enough to finish first in the tough AL East. Boston won 108 and had to face the Yankees in the Division Series. They did. They only lost once.

In addition to the games that Benny won with a bat in 2018, he also saved several with his glove. He made some spectacular plays on defense, including two in the postseason that should remain fixtures in highlight reels forever.

It was apparent that he was having fun with the Red Sox. Apparently, Brock Holt has always been very active on Instagram, and Benintendi made it a practice to add some comment every time Holt posted something. It became a running joke between them. Jackie Bradley Jr. was actually the most active on the team in interacting with fans through social media. "I have fun with it," he told Peter Abraham. "I'm not going to hide because some people are negative. This is part of the world we live in now."[15]

Benintendi had finally cut his hair over the winter, before the 2018 season. He'd also added another five pounds of muscle to his compact frame. And his dad helped him find a new agent, his previous agent having been suspended for secretly filming some of his clients in the shower. Benintendi had a 12-game hitting streak in spring training, but he really struggled once the season began.

Benny had the second of his game-winners—again victimizing the Yankees' Severino—with a triple on April 10 at Fenway. But he had failed to get a hit in his first 15 plate appearances and it wasn't until April 10 that he finally cracked .200. At the end of April, he was only hitting .242—though he did have an impressive 15 RBIs.

He poured it on in May batting .349 and driving in 23 runs, and finished that month at .299. He booked seven game-winners in 17 days, from May 17 through June 2. There were seven games in which he hit safely three times. You can build up your average pretty quickly with a blazing-hot stretch like that.

On June 6, he hit another game-winner, his eighth in a 21-day run.

On July 7 and 8, in back-to-back games in Kansas City, he reeled off this string that saw him reach base safely 10 plate appearances in a row: BB, BB, BB, BB, HR, 2B, and then 1B, 1B, 1B, 2B.

As his confidence grew, Benny's defensive exploits were becoming equally noteworthy. He played left field with total concentration, often sacrificing his body to make run-saving catches. In fact, in a game at Tampa Bay on August 22, he made what John Healy of the *New York Daily News* said at the time might be the play of the year. To the dismay of Rays fans, he nearly flipped over Tropicana Field's left-field fence to rob what would have been a two-run home run for Steven Souza Jr.

He had handled 56 chances with only one error, a remarkable feat for a player more accustomed to center field. He had only played four games in left field for Portland, and now was faced with playing half his games with a Green Monster looming over him. At the same time, he had to familiarize himself with the quirky, and sometimes downright bizarre, features of Fenway's left field.

Benny was a popular player, a fact easily confirmed by observing the sartorial choices of fans entering Fenway Park. At the end of

September, figures released by Major League Baseball reported that of online baseball jersey sales, Benintendi ranked No. 16 in all of baseball. Betts was ranked fifth.[16]

The voting for the Gold Gloves, of course, occurred before heading into the postseason. Before the results were announced, many thought it possible the Red Sox outfield would sweep. As it happens, Messrs. Betts and Bradley each were awarded a Gold Glove, but Benintendi was not. Given that he led the league in outfield assists (for the second year in a row), double plays turned as a left fielder, and Total Zone Runs as a left fielder, it wouldn't have surprised anyone had he, too, captured the coveted symbol of fielding excellence.

In Game One of the 2018 World Series, Benintendi got off to a hot start at Fenway against the visiting Los Angeles Dodgers, with a 4-for-5 night. It was only the third time in World Series history that a Red Sox player had recorded a four-hit game. He scored three of the Red Sox runs in an 8–4 victory, the first major leaguer to do so in his first World Series game. His response postgame? According to USA Today's A. J. Perez, he said, "I don't care, I'm just glad we won."[17]

He also had two highlight-reel catches during the postseason, on baseball's biggest stage. The first one probably saved a game. It came in Houston, in Game Four of the American League Championship Series. The Astros had won the first game, at Fenway, and then the Red Sox tied the series with a victory in Game Two. Game Three at Minute Maid Park also went to the Red Sox. If the Red Sox could win Game Four, they would go up three games to one, with three more opportunities to win the clinching game. It was a back-and-forth game. The Red Sox took an early 2–0 lead, and then 3–1 but the game was tied after three. The Astros took a 4–3 lead in the fourth. The Sox came back and tied it in the top of the fifth, but Houston reasserted its one-run lead in the bottom of the fifth. JBJ hit a two-run homer in the sixth, to tip it back, 6–5. The Sox added an insurance run in the seventh and another in the eighth, but the Astros got one back in the bottom of the eighth. Finally, it was 8–6 heading into the bottom of the ninth.

Manager Alex Cora had asked Craig Kimbrel to work two full innings. The power of hindsight suggests that he might have been asking too much. It was Kimbrel who was tagged for that one run in the bottom of the eighth. Alex Bregman, who he had hit with a pitch, and who advanced on George Springer's double, then came home on a grounder.

All Kimbrel needed to do was secure three outs, and to hold onto a two-run lead. The first Astro fouled out, but the bearded bullpen ace walked the next two, putting the tying runs on base. Brian McCann almost won the game with a drive to deep right field, but Betts hauled it in and there were two outs. With runners on first and third, Kimbrel walked yet another batter. The bases were loaded, and Bregman, an All-Star who would end up placing fifth in league MVP voting, was up again. On the first pitch from Kimbrel, Bregman hit a sinking line drive to left field. It looked like a sure base hit, which would at least bring in one run and maybe two to tie the game, given that the runners were off the minute bat hit ball. Benintendi might have played it safely and held them to one run, but he ran about 15 yards to his right and made a diving catch, just reaching, snaring, and holding on to the ball to end the game. As an excited TBS broadcaster said, "The guts it takes to make that play . . . if it gets by him, it's over." At the same split-second, Red Sox radio announcer Joe Castiglione's excited call of "He did it! He got it!" was followed by a thump and a barely audible "The Red Sox win!" The 72-year old Castiglione quickly recovered to explain "I just went head over heels in my chair."

Benintendi's second sensational postseason catch came in Game Two of the World Series, in Fenway Park, on October 24, 2018. The Red Sox had won the first game, 8–4. (In the bottom of the first, Benny singled and drove in Betts for the first run of the

Series.) In the second game, the Red Sox scored once in the second. But with David Price on the mound, the Dodgers came back with two in the fourth inning. They remained up, 2–1, when the fifth inning began. Leadoff batter Brian Dozier hit a ball that looked destined to hit off the lower part of the left-field wall. Benintendi ran to his right, leapt, and came down with the ball. It was perhaps easier than it looked, but the moment was captured forever in an iconic photograph that captured Benintendi in a running, leaping catch that had both feet maybe 2 ½ to 3 feet off the warning track. It was said that the resulting Jim Davis photograph channeled Nike's famous "Air Jordan" logo. Benintendi was, observed CBS Boston, "basically flying." The play was also captured in an ice sculpture, but for most Sox fans it is frozen for eternity in their mind's eye.

With three unanswered runs after making two outs in the bottom of the fifth, set up by Benintendi's eight-pitch walk that loaded the bases, the Red Sox won the game, 5–2.

The Red Sox dropped the marathon 18-inning-long Game Three (imagine the sacrifice LA fans had to make to stay up and watch a game that lasted until after midnight!), but came back and won Game Four and then Game Five to capture their fourth World Series of this century.

In December, Benny's catch of Bregman's line drive was deemed the Associated Press's "Play of the Year"—not just in baseball but in all of professional sports.[18] Among the profusion of measurement devices at work during major-league games these days, are "catch-probablilty" ratings. Statcast rated that Benintendi catch at a 21 percent probability, although in his own mind, the likelihood was close to 100 percent. It marked the lowest catch probability of any catch Benintendi made in 2018, but he told Masslive.com Christopher Smith, "I feel like I've made that catch before."[19]

"I was definitely excited. It's probably the most emotion I've shown on the field," Benintendi added. "Never get too high, never get too low. But yeah, maybe because that situation was during the playoffs." It put the Sox up three games to one. "But no, I wouldn't have dove if I didn't think I was going to catch it or there was any doubt in my mind at all. Yeah, I was pumped."

For the regular season, Benny was steady statistically. He drove in three fewer runs (87) but scored 103 runs as compared to the 84 he had scored in 2017. In part, that was due to getting on base more frequently—upping his batting average from .271 to .290 and his on-base percentage from .352 to .366. His fielding remained solid and consistent with that of the prior year. He was adept on the basepaths as well; he stole 20 bases in 25 attempts. It turns out that only two Red Sox ballplayers (Ellis Burks in 1987 and Nomar Garciaparra in 1997) have had rookie seasons in which they homered 20 or more times and stole 20 or more bases.

The Swing

Andrew Benintendi's swing turns even cynical, hard-bitten baseball men into shameless gushers. They describe his swing in the kind of glowing terms usually reserved for loved ones: beautiful, flawless, natural. Add to this, Benny's passion for hitting, his desire to improve, his intelligence, and his ability to lay off bad pitches, and you have to entertain the thought that he could be another . . . wait, surely this is heresy. These words may someday be the subject of scorn and ridicule. The thought of Benintendi—or anyone else—challenging Ted Williams in the hitting department is laughable. Sure, he plays the same left-field position and plays it with more skill than Ted did. Sure, he has more speed to get to balls and a better arm to peg the ball back to the infield. But in the same class as the Kid, the Splinter, Teddy Ballgame? Not yet.

Entire volumes have been written on the best way to hit a baseball. Benintendi has reduced his approach to its essence: "It's simple," he told Alex Speier of the *Boston Globe* in early 2017. "It's A to B."[20] There's beauty in simplicity. It's a textbook swing with no wasted motion and few variables. Ted Williams, the man who literally wrote the textbook on the subject, *The Science of Hitting*, would almost certainly have given him an A+ for summarizing his 100-page treatise into four words. Ted's advice to this young hitter would no doubt have been, "Don't let anyone change that swing." Ted passed on his hitting knowledge to generations of hitters from Mickey Mantle to Al Kaline to Wade Boggs to Mike Piazza. He did it in his book and he did it with his colorful preaching of the Golden Rules of hitting and 6-degree upswings.

Many have compared Benny's swing to that of Fred Lynn. While they are both things of beauty, Lynn believes they are fundamentally different. "I know that they've compared Benny's swing to mine, but our swings are different because he has short, compact arms and I have really long arms for my body. My arm length is that of someone six-two or six-three. So I had a real long, fluid swing and his is short and compact, like Rico Petrocelli's from the right side. Rico's was very similar to Benny's. Just cut the ball off. Mine was real long. Now it looked real smooth because I had pretty good bat speed even with that long swing. But they are different swings."

Boston's hitting coach Tim Hyers knew right away that Benny was a special kind of hitter when he first came across him in Lowell. "I just saw him that first year, but it was so easy to see that . . . just a natural swing. He made really good adjustments in game. Even to today—last year, 2018—the guy who made the most in-game adjustments in his favor was Andrew Benintendi. He's well beyond his years. He's like a guy who's got six or seven years under his belt, the adjustments he made—mentally and physically—to compete. He also has that sweet, natural-looking swing.

"I remember him coming in to Lowell, and it was like 'Wow!' He's not a big guy, but the ball just has an extra gear when he hits it. It just takes off. I thought, 'OK, this guy's going to be special.' He plays really good defense. He started out really slow. I think he put a lot of pressure on himself. Those high-profile guys who come out of the draft, there's just so much pressure on them. They're having to perform every day, because the scouts are there in practice. I don't think they're used to that. Then you get drafted, you sign, and then you take a little time off. It's like starting over again. Trying to perform, and you're playing with a lot of guys who went through spring training and the season. They're already prepared and in pro ball. I think he started a little slow. And he was tired. He just had that look the first couple of weeks. There was excitement, first pick with the Red Sox and all the stuff you have to go through, but he looked a little tired. Then he slid into home plate and hurt his thumb and it gave him about seven to ten days off. When he came back from that rest, he was a different guy. He needed that little break to kind of reset, catch his breath. I don't think he's ever stopped hitting from then on.

"I remember asking the Lowell coach, 'Is he OK? What's going on?' He said, 'His swing's fine. The numbers don't show it right now, but he just needs a little break and he'll be fine.' It was fun to watch."

Does Tim think Benintendi can become a consistent .300 hitter with maybe 25-home run power?

"Benny can do anything. That would not surprise me. He needs to use the whole field. His swing works that way. At some point during the year, I remember reading or hearing people talking that he had more opposite-field base hits than anybody in baseball at that point in the year. He just went after it. His swing works to all fields. He really works to the big part now. I do think he gets in trouble a little bit when he tries to spin off and create some power. That's what he did last year. He's always on base. He can run. He's a really good baserunner. All three of them, they have instincts in the outfield and they have instincts on the basepaths. He just causes so much trouble for the pitcher. And then here comes the big boys behind him and it's just Murderer's Row.

"I've never talked to a pitcher who loves to pitch with people on base. They hate it—and especially with someone who can run. They just want to get the ball and concentrate on their pitch. Throw the ball. Have that nice, easy delivery and execute a pitch. When you've got somebody on base, they've got to try and control the running game. We will never know how many times they've rushed the pitcher, or caused the pitcher to elevate a pitch. He's worried about the baserunner and he rushes through his delivery. He releases it high and doesn't get all the way through and leaves it up in the zone for J. D. or some of the other guys to capitalize on. We'll never know, but you watch the game, watch the pitchers, and we know that it affects them."

Without a moment's hesitation, Andrew frequently names his father as his most important baseball influence and yet Chris Benintendi takes no credit for his son's swing. Chris, the son of Sicilian emigrants, started lobbing tennis balls to Benny when he was 5, and went on to coach most of Andrew's teams from age eight to 13. "More than anything, he stressed the mental side of the game," said the younger Benintendi. "He would teach me just to mentally stay there." His father agrees: "I think my impact on Andrew, probably more than anything, is just the emotional part of things, handling success and failure."[21]

But when the subject turns to The Swing, Chris Benintendi is careful to point out that he deserves none of the credit. "I wish I could say something that was insightful about Andrew's swing or hitting in general," the elder Benintendi told us before the start of the 2019 season. "However, here is the hard truth: Andrew was born with that swing. At no point during his youth, amateur ball, or pro ball has anyone tinkered with that swing, including his old man. The swing you see today is the same swing he had at five years old. I take no credit for the swing. I never paid one dollar for hitting lessons. I guess I should consider myself lucky, but I was smart enough to leave the swing alone. Over the years we have discussed other parts of hitting, like hand position, open/closed stance, and the dreaded leg kick. As you know, timing is key and all the above play a part."

Because Benny's swing has often been compared to Ted Williams's, it's natural to assume that Chris might have gotten some of his hitting philosophy from *The Science of Hitting*. Not so. "I never saw Ted Williams play," Chris says, adding that his personal hitting heroes played for the Cincinnati Reds of the 1970s. "I was spoiled by the Big Red Machine when I was a kid growing up in the country an hour from Riverfront Stadium. Hopefully, Andrew will continue to improve and become the best hitter he can be. His calling card has always been his bat and I hope the best is yet to come. He will give his best. Anyway, I hope he continues to swing the bat to where he draws such favorable comparisons."

Benintendi confirms that his swing was self-created and not the product of professional instruction "I've never taken a lesson or anything like that," Benintendi told Alex Speier in April of 2017. "I've never really needed to, and hopefully I'll never have to.

"I don't remember [losing my swing] happening any time because it's so simple. The swing has always been the same," he continued. "When I'm struggling, it might be timing or pitch recognition, but I'll never go back and change my swing. There's nothing to change. It's so simple. I think that's helped a lot. When I'm not going well, I know it's my timing, but not my swing."[22]

Chris Benintendi is to be commended for what he didn't do. He didn't tamper with his son's natural swing. The instinct for any parent is to instruct and correct. The tough part is to let the kids discover something by trial and error and not interfere. Even though he had played collegiate baseball, he was wise enough to allow his son to create his own swing and then devoted and insightful enough to bolster his belief in it.

"When it came to mechanics and getting from A to B, it was, don't waste any motion," Chris said. "What I've learned over the years is that for anyone to make it to the highest levels of the major leagues, you've got to start with hitting a fastball. If you can't hit a fastball, you have no chance of making it.

"[But] I didn't teach him that swing. That was a God-given swing that he had, really ever since he started swinging a bat. I was probably the first of many people who didn't screw it up."

Nevertheless, you don't get points for a pretty swing if you fail to make regular contact with the ball. Benintendi's approach at the plate was devised to do make that happen—a lot. Benintendi's stance is upright and open. There's no exaggerated pre-pitch routine, no hitting tics, no hesitation. His hand-eye coordination is excellent and he's blessed with strong wrists and quick hands. His goal is to use these physical attributes to maximum effect. The swing is pure, simple, and compact—the quickest way between two points—and the leg lift is minimal. His bat control and bat speed allow him to hit to all fields. This, coupled with superior pitch recognition and knowledge of the strike zone, gives him the luxury of patience, even when the count is against him. He usually makes contact and seldom strikes out. His newly-added bulk allows him to pull the ball to the fences in deep right field or in center and if he's pitched outside, he can poke the ball to left or off the wall for a double.

Despite the fact that they bat from different sides of the plate, Fred Lynn sees similarities between Benintendi and his former teammate Jim Rice. "I played with Jimmie in the minors so I've known him since he was 20, and he could always hit. He couldn't always catch the ball. Even in the minors that was a work in progress. But he could always hit. It was just something he could do and Jimmie was bigger and stronger than everybody. He had massive arms on him and the ball just came off the bat differently that everybody else. I see Benny as a compact, lefty version of Jimmie, or [Rico] Petrocelli. As left-handed hitters—Jackie and Benny are going to have success if their first thought is left-center all the time. Left-center! Left-center! Left-center! What that allows you to do is wait on the ball longer. When you hit the ball the other way, it's in the air, not on the ground, so now you've got to take advantage of the wall or hit them into the net [editor's note: the net is no more, replaced by the Monster seats]. And those kinds of strategies and techniques pay off when you go on the road because now you're locked in and you don't have two different swings, one at Fenway and another on the road. You just lock into that one swing and you'll be better off for it."

Lynn predicts a bright future for Benintendi. "Benny is a good hitter and he's going to be even better," he says. "He's going to hit right around .300 consistently because he runs well. He doesn't strike out a lot from what I've seen. I don't see a ton of games, but I'm back there [Boston] for 15 or 16 games a year so I get to see him a little bit. Like I say, he has a compact swing so he's got a little power and that power will kind of manifest at weird times. He may be a streaky home run hitter. I do know he loves hitting at Yankee Stadium, with that short porch. He does well there. Maybe he changes his philosophy when he goes there. But he has the ability to be a 20-home run guy, that's for sure. So he can hit .280 to .300, around there, and above that in a good year—bad years, maybe .270. He shouldn't go below that because he's too good a hitter. He has too good an idea. Home runs, anywhere from 15 to 25 and who knows, if he figures it out, he could get to 30."

The Glove

Comparisons in left field begin with Yaz. He would never match Ted Williams as a hitter, but even Ted granted that he played left field like no one ever had before or since. His ability to play caroms off the wall and decoy runners was an art form. The batter would hit the ball toward the wall and run to first and as he rounded the bag, he'd see Yaz, hands on hips looking up at the wall as if it had been a homer. He'd slow his stride. The next thing you knew, Yaz had played the carom, wheeled around, and gunned the poor sap out at second.

He had a thousand strategies and in the course of his career, he used them all.

Observers see flashes of Yaz when Benintendi takes the field. With Jackie Bradley Jr. roaming center and Mookie Betts guarding right, latecomer Benintendi was left to play the most unique left field in baseball. Fenway's left field gives visiting outfielders fits and a potential home field advantage—but only if you learn to play it better than your visiting counterpart. Benny worked hard to learn the quirks of his domain. He quickly learned that to be effective he had to think like a pool player to anticipate the caroms off the wall. He had to sense the proximity of the wall and anticipate early on which balls could be caught and which should be played on the rebound. He had to learn to pivot and peg those caroms to second to cut down an overconfident runner.

It wasn't only hitting that young Andrew learned while playing in the yard with his dad. Catching the ball was also part of the fun. Chris Benintendi made it interesting by using his tennis raquet to rocket tennis balls high into the air.

"We didn't know any better," Chris Benintendi told Alex Speier. "Now I see someone five years old. One thing I might think in my own mind is, do I think this young boy could catch a ball towering 100 feet or 200 feet in the air? The answer is probably no. But he was able to do it."[23]

"He moves at a different pace than a lot of people on the field in terms of how he processes information on the baseball field," added Red Sox scout Chris Mears.[24]

It's a long way from the Benintendi backyard to Fenway's left field, but the lessons he learned there are what placed him on the path to the majors.

His second major-league season was now over and he was a key member of a World Series-championship team. Pausing for a moment to consider 2017 Rookie of the Year Aaron Judge, in his 112 games (he missed a portion of the season due to injury), he still struck out 152 times compared to Benintendi's 106 strike-outs in 151 games. His homers dropped nearly 50 percent—from 52 down to 27. He had 67 RBIs compared to Benintendi's 87. In terms of sophomore seasons, it was no contest. There is no Sophomore of the Year Award, but Benintendi could care less. He was the proud owner of a World Series ring.

Benintendi's Outfield Assists
Benintendi's 11 outfield assists were the most by a Red Sox rookie since Carl Yastrzemski (also 11) in 1961. He led the league in assists by a left fielder.

Not only did he tie for leading the majors in outfield assists in 2018, with 12, but six times he earned that assist leading to a runner being thrown out at home plate—something he had done three times in 2017. In 2018:

April 3, at Miami. His single in the top of the 11th had given the Red Sox a 2–1 lead but the Marlins got two runners on base when Cameron Maybin doubled to deep left. One run scored, tying the game, 2–2. Benintendi's throw to Xander Bogaerts, who then fired to Christian Vázquez, cut down Justin Bour at the plate and prevented the Marlins from winning the game. In the 13th he was walked intentionally and then scored the second of two Red Sox runs when Hanley Ramirez doubled. The Sox won, 4–2.

May 8 at New York. The Sox and Yanks were tied, 2–2, in the bottom of the seventh. The Yankees had the bases loaded and Aaron Judge at the plate. Judge singled to left field, and one run scored, but Benintendi's throw to the plate prevented runner, Gleyber Torres, who was on second base, from scoring. New York won that game, 3–2, but Benintendi had kept it a one-run game.

May 13 at Toronto. Just five days later, another baserunner tried to score on him. The Sox held a 4–3 lead in the bottom of the seventh. The Blue Jays had Yangervis Solarte on first base with two outs. Russell Martin doubled to left. Solarte made the mistake of going for an extra 90 feet and was erased when Bogaerts relayed Benny's throw to the plate. The 4–3 score stood at game's end.

June 5, at Fenway Park against the Detroit Tigers. This erasure came in the top of the first inning. Leonys Martin led off the game with a walk. The second batter, Nick Castellanos, doubled to deep left-center. Martin tried to score on Benny's arm. He failed. Benintendi threw him out on another relay via Bogaerts to Vázquez at the plate. Benintendi led off for the Red Sox, singled, and scored on a J. D. Martinez home run. Benny's run was the winning run; the Red Sox ultimately won, 6–0.

July 23, at Baltimore. The Red Sox had a 1–0 lead in the bottom of the fourth. Jace Peterson walked. With two outs, he tried to make it home on Jonathan Schoop's long double to left-center. Nothing doing. Benintendi threw him out, via X-Man at short. The Sox won the game, 5–3, with Benintendi's two-run ground-rule double in the top of the fifth accounting for their third and fourth runs of the game.

September 5, at Atlanta. The Braves were leading the game, 2–1, as they came up to bat in the bottom of the fourth. Lucas Duda walked. With one out, Tyler Flowers doubled down the left-field line. Duda tried to score, but his attempt was in vain. Benintendi's throw to Brock Holt at short and Holt's throw to Christian Vázquez were both on the money. Duda was out. The Red Sox won the game, 9–8, coming from behind in the top of the ninth when Benintendi singled and Brandon Phillips followed with a home run.

Andrew Benintendi's Game-Winning Hits (through 2018)

August 14, 2016: Noted in the Mookie Betts section, this was the game in which Betts had eight RBIs and the Red Sox beat the Diamondbacks, 16–2. Betts could have had 100 RBIs, though, and the game-winning hit still would have belonged to Andrew Benintendi. Playing in his 11th big-league game, he had already booked five career RBIs, but in the bottom of the second inning of this game, facing Zack Greinke, with runners on first and second and nobody out, Benintendi doubled to right field and drove in the third Red Sox run. (Betts had hit a two-run homer in the first to kick things off.) It was the third run that won the game.

September 22, 2016: The Sox got one in the top of the first, and two in the top of the second. The Orioles scored thrice in the bottom of the third to tie it. In the top of the fifth, Travis Shaw walked on six pitches. Baltimore's Vance Worley struck out JBJ and Sandy Leon. A wild pitch with Benintendi batting allowed Shaw to take second base. He singled to right field, scoring Shaw, but was himself thrown out trying to stretch his single to two bases. No matter; the run had scored. It was the fourth run in a 5–3 win.

April 3, 2017: Opening Day, 2017. The Pittsburgh Pirates, of all teams, were at Fenway Park. Neither squad scored for the first half of the game. In the bottom of the fifth inning, Pablo Sandoval singled in the first run of the season and Dustin Pedroia singled in the second. And then Benintendi homered to left field. 5–0, Red Sox. The Pirates clawed back three runs, but it wasn't enough.

April 18, 2017: Every run counts in an 8–7 win. The Red Sox were in Toronto, where the Jays took a 2–0 lead in the first. The Sox went up 3–2 in the third. The Jays tied it. The Red Sox added three more in the fifth. Betts homered to lead off the seventh and they were up, 7–4. In the top of the eighth, Benintendi hit a ball to deep center that went for a ground-rule double, scoring Sandoval, who had been on second base. Seeing as how the Blue Jays scored three times in the bottom of the ninth, that eighth run made all the difference.

June 6, 2017: The Red Sox built up a 5–1 lead at Yankee Stadium. The fifth run came courtesy of a Masahiro Tanaka offering, which Benintendi hit into the Stadium's short right-field porch. The Yankees scored three later runs—one on a double play and one on a strikeout/wild pitch. Thus, the Sox's fifth run was the difference-maker.

June 13, 2017: The night before, the Red Sox beat the Phillies, 6–5, in the bottom of the 11th. This night, the Sox scored single runs in the first, second, and third. The Phils got two in the third and one in the sixth, and here we were in extra innings again. In the bottom of the 12th, Pedroia grounded out, Bogaerts drew a walk, Mitch Moreland singled to left with Bogaerts going first to third, and then Benintendi got the barrel of water poured all over him after he singled to right to win the game in another walk-off.

July 3, 2017: Dustin Pedroia had a two-run double and then a two-run single. The Red Sox took a 5–4 lead into the bottom of the ninth in Texas. They called on ace closer Craig Kimbrel to save the game, but he let former Red Sox player Mike Napoli homer to tie the game. In the top of the 11th, a walk, a double, and an intentional walk set the stage for Benintendi (who had entered the game as a pinch-hitter for Chris Young in the top of the ninth). Benintendi singled in two runs. Heath Hembree got the win.

July 4, 2017: The very next night, still playing the Rangers, the Sox put up 11 runs, scoring reasonably early and reasonably often. The Rangers got four. The fifth (and sixth and seventh) runs of the game came thanks to a three-run homer by Mr. Benintendi off Yu Darvish in the top of the fifth.

July 14, 2017: After the All-Star Break, the Yankees paid a visit to Fenway Park. It was a seesaw game early, and New York catcher Gary Sanchez played a big part in that, with three RBIs. From the fifth inning on, the Yankees held a 4–3 lead. Then Aroldis Chapman came in to close in the bottom of the ninth, at which point he gave up singles to Betts and Pedroia. With Bogaerts at the plate, they pulled off a double steal. Unnerving, no doubt. Bogaerts then hit the ball to second baseman Ronald Torreyes, who committed his second error of the game, while Betts scored the tying run from third. Chapman walked Hanley Ramirez intentionally to load the bases and set up a play at any base. There was no play; Chapman walked Benintendi on five pitches. "Dirty Water" started playing throughout the park.

August 5, 2017: The White Sox scored once in the top of the first inning. They never scored again. Drew Pomeranz threw 6 ⅓ innings, then turned it over to the bullpen. The Red Sox scored twice in the first (a two-run homer by Benintendi over the Red Sox bullpen and into the bleachers) and twice in the second. That was more than enough. It was his first homer since the Fourth of July.

August 12, 2017: During a late Saturday afternoon game at Yankee Stadium, the Red Sox scored five runs in the third inning and five more in the fifth. That was plenty; the Yankees only scored five more in the entire game. The first five Sox runs came on a two-run single by Betts and a three-run homer by Benintendi. The second five came on another three-run homer by Benintendi (both off Luis Severino) and a two-run double by Rafael Devers.

August 13, 2017: Sunday night baseball followed a day later. This one went into extra innings. Each team scored one run in the fifth inning. The Yanks took a 2–1 lead in the bottom of the eighth. Devers homered off Chapman to tie it back up in the top of the ninth. Chapman struck out Moreland in the top of the 10th, but then he hit Bradley and walked Nuñez. New York manager Joe Girardi figured Chapman was losing it, so he summoned Tommy Kahnle to take over. Kahnle walked Betts to load the bases, and then surrendered a single to Benintendi. Kimbrel put down the Yankees 1-2-3.

September 18, 2017: The Orioles seemed to be on a roll for their home fans, racking up the runs early on—one in the first, three in the second, one more in the third, and another one in the fourth. The Red Sox got one in the fourth, but for Orioles fans it had to be disappointing to see the Red Sox score six runs in the top of the fifth, momentarily taking the lead. But the O's came back with two more in their half of the fifth. Bogaerts tied it with a leadoff homer in the top of the seventh. Neither team scored in the next three innings. In the top of the 11th, Red Sox batters grounded out, walked, grounded out, and then took an intentional walk. A completely unintentional walk followed that, Tzu-Wei Lin working through eight pitches to earn it. Then Benintendi singled and drove in two. Carson Smith induced three infield grounders to end the O's hopes in the bottom of the 11th.

April 8, 2018: Andrew Benintendi recorded an incredible 15 game-winning hits in 2018. The first came on April 8, when the Rays scored at least one run in every inning from the second through the seventh. They led, 7–2, Rays heading into the bottom of the eighth. Benintendi was the ninth Boston batter in the eighth and drove in the sixth run of the inning with a double to center field. The rally had begun with two outs and a runner on second. Then followed six consecutive hits, including Benintendi's game-winner which made it 8–7, Red Sox. Kimbrel induced three infield outs. Game over.

April 10, 2018: The first meeting with the Yankees in 2018 saw the Sox win at home, 14–1. The BoSox got one in the first, and then the only other runs they truly needed with three in the second inning. With runners on first and second, Benintendi tripled off

Severino, driving the ball to deep right. Mookie's grand slam in the sixth was pure icing, on the icing, on the cake. Chris Sale booked his first win.

April 30, 2018: Eddy Rodriguez granted the Royals three runs in the top of the first, and a couple more in the fourth. Moreland hit a solo homer in the second, then walked in Benintendi on a bases-loaded pass in the third. Bogaerts followed that with a grand slam. In the fourth, JBJ walked and Christian Vázquez singled. With men on first and third, Benintendi hit a sacrifice fly to make it 8–7, Red Sox. Two later insurance runs served just that purpose, but the sac fly was the game-winner.

May 17, 2018: Another sacrifice fly won another game at Fenway Park. This one came in the bottom of the fourth against the Orioles. Bradley walked, then stole second. Betts singled. Benintendi hit a Kevin Gausman pitch deep enough to right field to score JBJ. That made it 3–0, Red Sox. Three batters later, Bogaerts drove Gausman from the game with a three-run homer. The final score was 6–2, a complete game from David Price.

May 19, 2018: Then followed the second of seven game-winners in 17 days. The Red Sox won 16 of 19 games against the Orioles in 2018. They won this one by a 6–3 score. It was 1–1 at the midpoint but in the bottom of the fifth, Betts hit a two-run homer off Dylan Bundy into the Monster seats. Benintendi followed that with a solo home run into the Orioles bullpen. That made it 4–1. The Sox never surrendered the lead. There is no record as to what the Orioles may have done with Benintendi's home run ball.

May 25, 2018: The visiting Atlanta Braves scored twice in the third, and the Red Sox matched those two runs in the bottom of the fourth on solo homers from J. D. Martinez and Xander Bogaerts. In the fifth, JBJ tripled and after Betts drew a walk, Benintendi hit a sacrifice fly to deep left-center, giving the Sox a 3–2 lead. They won in the end, 6–2, courtesy of a two-run homer by Mookie and a solo one by Mitch Moreland. The only Red Sox run that didn't come via homer was Benintendi's, but it was the one that won the game.

May 26, 2018: The next afternoon, the Braves scored six runs, but the Red Sox topped that with eight. The Red Sox had a 6–5 lead after six innings. In the bottom of the seventh, Benintendi (who had hit a solo home run to lead off the fourth) tripled with Nuñez (reached on error) and Betts (walked) aboard. Now it was 8–5. Ronald Acuna homered off Kimbrel in the top of the ninth, but it didn't make any difference in the outcome. It was Benintendi's eighth three-hit game of the still-young season.

May 28, 2018: One can't have a game-winner if your team loses the game. Dropping a game to Atlanta, 6–1, there was no game-winner on the 27th, but on the 28th, things picked back up again and for the third consecutive Red Sox win, it was Benintendi who led the way, with yet another three-hit game. The game-winner was a three-run homer—the first one in his career that he had hit to left field in Fenway. Final: Red Sox 8, Blue Jays 3.

June 2, 2018: The Sox (managed by Alex Cora) were in Houston, playing the 2017 world champions, whom he had coached in 2017. Boston lost the first game of the doubleheader, 7–3. On Saturday night, June 2, they won, 5–4, thanks to three runs in the top of the seventh. Christian Vázquez homered to tie it, 3–3, and then Bradley walked. Benintendi homered deep into the second deck in right field.

June 6, 2018: This was the eighth game-winner for Benintendi in just three weeks (21 days). He was 2-for-5 with a double and a home run. It was his third-inning double that was the game-winner. The homer leading off the bottom of the fifth made it 5–1. The final score was Red Sox 7, Tigers 1.

July 23, 2018: The victim was Baltimore's Gausman. Betts already had two game-winners off him, one in 2016 and one in 2017. This was Benintendi's second off him (see also May 17, 2018). It was a two-out, two-run ground-rule double in the top of the fifth inning, at Camden Yards. The Sox won, 5–3.

August 5, 2018: A fun game for fans at Fenway Park. The Yankees took a 4–1 lead in the top of the seventh (that wasn't the fun part). In the bottom of the ninth, Aroldis Chapman struck out the side—but not before walking three batters, allowing a single, and seeing an error by Miguel Andujar, which all combined to see the Sox send the game into extra innings. That was more fun. In the bottom of the 10th, Jonathan Holder took over. He got the first two batters on a strikeout and a groundout, respectively, but then allowed a single, threw a wild pitch, and walked Mookie intentionally. Benintendi then singled right up the middle. That occasioned a lot of fun for most of those present.

August 10, 2018: Combining for 31 runs on 33 hits, the Red Sox outlasted the Orioles, 19–12. Bogaerts had four RBIs, and Holt, Betts, and Benintendi each had three. It was Benintendi's three-run homer in the top of the seventh that catapulted the Red Sox into a 14–10 lead at the time, enough to win the game.

August 22, 2018: The Red Sox beat the Indians handily, 10–4, at Fenway Park. That magical fifth run crossed the plate in the person of Blake Swihart in the bottom of the fourth inning. He was the middle man of three (Holt first, and Betts third), all of whom scored on Benintendi's double that cleared the bases.

September 16, 2018: The "other" New York team—the Mets—came to Boston in mid-September. The Red Sox lost the first game of three, 8–0, then won the second, 5–3. This Sunday afternoon game proved to be a one-run affair. The Sox took a 3–0 lead off Jacob deGrom in the bottom of the third, but the Mets tied it up with two runs in the sixth and one in the seventh. In the bottom of the eighth, Tzu-Wei Lin doubled. He tagged and went to third on Holt's fly ball to deep center field, and then tagged up and scored on Benintendi's sacrifice fly to more or less the same place in deep right-center.

Benintendi had 15 game-winning hits for the Red Sox in 2018 (four on sacrifice flies), far more than the nine that Betts had or the eight Bradley had. Like them, however, he has yet to have a game-winning hit in postseason play.

Andrew Benintendi is the guy you want at the plate when there are runners in scoring position. Through the 2018 season, he batted

.341 with RISP, driving in 149 runs in 382 plate appearances. Even when he didn't drive in a run with a base hit, he still got himself on base. His on-base percentage was .441. When there were runners in scoring position and two outs, he was even more productive, batting .381. One way or another, he got on base almost exactly half the time—a .494 OBP. Conclusion? When there are ducks are on the pond, Benny goes above and beyond.

Jackie Bradley Jr., Center Field

Despite the generational suffix attached to his name, Jackie Bradley Jr. is actually the senior partner in the prestigious fielding firm of Benintendi, Bradley, and Betts. Jackie arrived in Boston's outfield in 2013, a year before Mookie Betts debuted in right field and three years before Andrew Benintendi began transitioning into his duties in left. With these three glove men on the job, the defense never rests for the Red Sox and center fielder Bradley is especially busy, recording 326 putouts in 2018 alone. In that championship season, he committed only six errors, recorded nine outfield assists, and doubled up three baserunners, while posting a fielding average of .982. He also won his first Gold Glove at a position blessed with a number of outstanding challengers.

Largely because of his stellar defense, Jackie's arrival in Boston had been greatly anticipated. In fact, ever since the day his mom was taken by police cruiser to the hospital delivery room to give birth to him, JBJ's arrivals have created a great deal of commotion. The police escort was courtesy of her colleagues at the Virginia Department of Corrections where she worked.

Six months earlier, Alfreda Hagans had come very close to miscarrying the future Gold Glove center fielder. At the time, she was doing 12-hour shifts as a police officer. "The doctor immediately told me, 'You're on the verge of losing this baby. We don't know

if he's going to make it. We have to take you off your feet immediately,'" Hagans told Christopher Smith in May 2018.[25] The bed
rest did the trick and, six months later, it was time for JBJ to enter
the world. But he seemed reluctant to do so. It took 19 hours of
labor before he finally showed up on April 19, 1990.

Bradley is not ashamed to wear his emotions on his sleeve,
or on his back. Partly as a tribute to his mother's painful birthing
experience, his uniform number became 19. In fact, Jackie's jersey is an homage to both of his parents. He insisted that the name
on his back be Bradley Jr. in order to recognize his father, Jackie
Bradley Sr., who in turn had been given the name in honor of soul
singer Jackie Wilson.

"He's Senior, and I'm his son and I'm just trying to go out
and honor him," he told Ian Browne of *MLB.com* in June of 2016.
"When he was younger, he liked playing baseball a lot, and he obviously played basketball in college. He kind of feels like he's living
through me vicariously, because this is what he wanted to do when
he was younger."[26]

"I've always wanted it there," Bradley added. "A lot of people
say, 'Oh, you don't need Junior,' and I'd say, 'You don't need to
focus on my last name.' It's just something I've grown to like. It's
like it's a part of me now."

In lighter moments, Jackie Jr. suggests there was also a less
sentimental reason for drawing the distinction between father and
son. "My dad used to say, 'I'm not going to go to jail for you and
you're not going to jail for me, so make sure you put Junior on your
stuff and I'll put Senior on mine and that way there's no confu-
sion.'" Mistaken identities aside, his father appreciates the gesture
of respect. "I'm Senior. I'm the one that made him," said Bradley
Sr. "It makes me feel proud that [my] son is out there as Junior."

Honoring others is important to Jackie. Next time he goes up
to bat, watch him closely. Before he enters the box, he uses his bat
to carefully form two capital M's in the dirt. Not until this task is
complete does he step in to hit. The first M is a tribute to his best
friend Matt Saye, who died tragically in a car accident in 2011 at

the age of 21. The two had been best buddies since the age of 10 and the loss hit Bradley hard. Saye's obituary made it clear just how close the two had been: "He is survived by his parents and his sister, Elizabeth Jane Saye of Nashville, Tenn., and his brother, Jackie Bradley Jr. of Prince George, Va."[27]

A second M began to appear after his beloved maternal grandmother Martha Brown passed away in April of 2014. She had encouraged him to pursue his baseball dreams since he was a little boy.

So the M's are for Matt and Martha and it's hard to imagine a more fitting tribute for two people who inspired him to be the very best. As he told Jonathon Seidl, editor-in-chief of the website *I Am Second*, "It's letting me know they have my back and are in full support of me."[28]

Jackie's work ethic can be traced to both parents, although he is hardly a clone of either. He and his mother have striking similarities, but their demeanors differ. The center fielder shows the deceptive calm in the core of a hurricane. Alfreda Hagans is the hurricane, or at least a whirlwind. She's worked as a corrections officer, a Virginia state trooper, an evangelist, a property manager, a restaurateur-caterer, and a marketer. Whatever the job, her primary focus was the kids, to make sure they "felt the love." "Just being there for them and knowing whatever aspirations they had in life, just to be there to support it."[29]

Jackie Sr. works as a bus driver for the Greater Richmond Transit Company and operates a lawn maintenance business on the side. He's always on the go, a fact that didn't go unnoticed by young Bradley "My dad . . . he kind of led by example," Bradley Jr. told Browne. "He's a hard worker—a real, real hard worker. He just tried to make sure that me, my brother [Dominique] and now my younger sister [Chyna] always stayed on the right path."

The couple divorced in 1997 just before Jackie Jr.'s seventh birthday, but they remain the cornerstones in his life. Jackie learned their lessons well. He has the fame and attention that comes with being a major leaguer in perspective. When he leaves the ballpark, he is Jackie Bradley Jr., husband and father. "Jackie's always talked about being a family man, even before he got married," his mother told Christopher Smith of *MassLive.com* in early 2018. "He pretty much already mapped out in his mind what he wanted life to be."[30]

"I'm able to separate the game from my family life and home life just because at the end of the day, it's just a game for me," he told Smith in 2015. "I enjoy playing it but it's not the end-all, be-all for me." JBJ makes it clear that his life goals are much larger than Gold Gloves or even world championships. "Just being a great man and living for God," he said. "That's where I keep my faith. Baseball is not going to make or break me."[31]

Jackie Bradley Jr. and Mookie Betts were both drafted on the same date (June 6, 2011). In the June 2011 amateur draft, Red Sox Director of Amateur Scouting Amiel Sawdaye and team GM Theo Epstein began selecting players to stock future Red Sox teams. The Red Sox had four picks in the first 40, due to the loss of both Victor Martinez and Adrian Beltre to free agency. Their first selection was Matt Barnes, taken in the first round (No. 19 overall) and their second was Blake Swihart (first round, 26th pick). The Barnes opportunity came from the Tigers as compensation for Martinez and Swihart came as compensation for Beltre signing with the Rangers.

In the supplemental first round, the Sox picked up two more future major leaguers: Henry Owens, No. 36 overall, and Jackie Bradley Jr., No. 40 (Owens for Martinez, and Bradley thanks to Beltre). Red Sox scout Quincy Boyd had followed Jackie and been his advocate.

In rounds two through four, the Sox selected Williams Jerez, Jordan Weems, and Noe Ramirez. In round five, the Red Sox selected Mookie Betts—as a shortstop. He was selection No. 172 overall. All but Jerez were given signing bonuses that were significantly greater than their slot positions. Bradley's slot called for him to receive $829,000, but the Red Sox gave him a bonus of $1,100,000. Betts's slot was pegged at $129,500, but he got $750,000, no doubt because the Sox needed to entice him away from following through on his commitment to play baseball for the University of Tennessee.

In May 2011, *Baseball America* had ranked Bradley No. 34 in the nation. Meanwhile, Betts had not yet made the top 200. After graduating from Prince George (Virginia) High School, Jackie attended the University of South Carolina. As a sophomore, he had been named Most Outstanding Player in the 2010 College World Series.

Coach Ray Tanner never had any doubt that Jackie was a special player. As Tanner said in an interview, "From the first time I saw him—I saw him playing in the summer when he was in high school for a team called the Richmond Braves, which was an AAU team. Even at that time, I was impressed with his grace as a player. You always hear in baseball that you can't be too high, you can't be too low. You've got to respect the game. You've got to play it the right way. It will humble you. He was the epitome of how you should approach the game. In my opinion.

"It's a hard game. Baseball's a hard game. And I'm watching that young player handle himself like a veteran. At the time, I guess he was probably 17.

"I was fortunate enough to lure him to the University of South Carolina. There wasn't any difference between his freshman year and his junior year when he ended up being a pick by the Red Sox. He just played the game the right way, every single day.

"His approach to practice was: no wasted time, efficiency, effectiveness. People talk about his defense. He did that in practice for us every single day. It wasn't like I was out there pushing him and shoving him in practice to make plays. That was just his investment. He would run routes, and he would react in batting practice."[32]

In college with the South Carolina Gamecocks, Bradley hit .349 as a freshman in 2009, showing some power with 11 home runs and a slugging percentage of .537. He batted left and threw right-handed. He played in New England for the first time that summer as a member of the Hyannis Mets (now the Hyannis Harbor Hawks) in the Cape Cod League, "where the stars of tomorrow shine tonight." Though the 16–26 Mets finished in last place, Bradley performed well, playing outfield and hitting for a .275 average in 43 games, tied for third on the team with 14 RBIs. When Jackie Bradley Jr. played for the Hyannis Mets, he was billeted in the home of Tino and Terri DiGiovanni. They were such great hosts that Bradley still drops in to see them and even invited them to his wedding. Terri confessed that she "liked everything about him," especially the fact that "he loved to eat."

As for Tino, he was instrumental in helping Jackie maintain a positive mental attitude as he went through the inevitable highs and lows of learning the game. Whatever he did obviously worked because despite regular offensive struggles with the Red Sox, Bradley has proven resilient and always maintained a quiet confidence in himself.

When their former charge was drafted by the Red Sox in 2011, both his birth family and extended family were thrilled, with one notable exception. Turns out Tino is a Yankee fan. "I told him I'd root for you, but the Red Sox—not so much." Tino would become especially torn in the midst of Jackie's 29-game hitting streak in 2016. He once texted him, "I'm going to baseball hell if this keeps up."[33]

Playing NCAA Division I baseball in the Southeastern Conference with the 2010 Gamecocks, Bradley helped the team place first, hitting .368 with 13 homers. In 67 college games that year, he drove in 60 runs. The Gamecocks went on to win the 2010 College World Series, beating UCLA in the finals, 7–1 and 2–1. JBJ hit .345 in the series with two homers and nine RBIs. They repeated as champions in 2011. Bradley, a sophomore, was 10-for-29 in 2010 and was named the Most Outstanding Player of the College World Series. Coach Tanner was named National Coach of the Year by both *Baseball America* and *Collegiate Baseball*.

Bradley contributed to the 2011 team as well but had struggled a bit in college play his junior year and injured his wrist in late April. He returned in time to make the final catch that clinched the national title for the Gamecocks again in 2011. "Yeah, he dove for a ball at Mississippi State," explained Coach Tanner. "A low liner got in front of him, and he had a wrist injury. But if you notice now, he gets his body clear before he makes that play. If he gets to a ball, he's going to catch it. You see a lot of outfielders get to balls and they don't catch it. If he gets to it, he's going to catch it."

Having been drafted by the Red Sox in June, Bradley went on to begin his pro career.

In the summer of 2011, once he had agreed to terms, JBJ played for two pro teams. On August 23, he returned to Massachusetts and played the first of six games for the Single-A Lowell Spinners. He walked and scored his first time up. All told, he had 25 plate appearances, with four base hits and four walks. He struck out five times and was caught stealing both times he attempted a steal, but he scored five runs. Most importantly, he got his feet wet professionally. After the Spinners' season ended on August 31, he returned to South Carolina and got into four games with the Greenville Drive (Class A South Atlantic League), where he went 5-for-15 with a home run and his first three RBIs as a pro. He played center field for both teams.

In 2012, JBJ played a full season of 128 games, split almost equally between two teams. For the Salem Red Sox in Virginia (Class A+ Carolina League), he played 67 games between April 6 and June 17, batting .359 with three homers and 34 RBIs. He drew 52 walks, too, and had a very impressive on-base percentage of .480. He was 16-for-22 in stolen base attempts.

For his stellar work in April, he had been named defensive player of the month in the Red Sox minor-league system. Through May 23, he was leading Salem, batting .367 with a .495 on-base percentage.

He was named a Carolina League All-Star and was leading the Red Sox organization with a .359 average, earning a promotion to the Portland Sea Dogs (Double A Eastern League) on June 25.

JBJ played out the rest of the season with Portland. At this higher level, he was more susceptible to the strikeout but hit .271 with six homers and 29 RBIs. He'd really done it all and was cited by *Baseball America* as the "best hitting prospect, baserunner, defensive outfielder, and most exciting player in the Carolina League."[34] The Red Sox knew center fielder Jacoby Ellsbury was a year away from free agency, and seemed to be constantly dogged by injuries. They were looking for someone to fill his shoes. In September, Bradley was named 2012 Defensive Player of the Year in the Red Sox minor-league system and received his award at Fenway Park on September 22, 2012. His performance that season had given the Red Sox hope that they would have a viable alternative to Jacoby Ellsbury when Ellsbury's contract expired at the end of the 2013 season.

Both Bradley and shortstop Xander Bogaerts were the targets of a number of teams seeking to acquire young talent from the Red Sox, but the team steadfastly refused to budge on who they considered their top two prospects.

At spring training in 2013 in Fort Myers, Bradley's uniform didn't seem to fit. Oh, the size was fine, carefully tailored to accommodate his 5-foot-10, 200-pound frame. It was the number that didn't fit. The number 74 just didn't suit Jackie Bradley Jr. It was a temporary number and everyone who saw him play that spring knew it, including Jackie, who had already expressed a preference for number 19 if he made the roster.

He opened many eyes during those spring sessions, with his bat and his glove. Christopher Gasper of the *Boston Globe* wrote, "Bradley tracks down balls as if his glove has GPS. He doesn't run them down. He casually meets up with them, relying on angles, intelligence, and instincts." Bradley told Gasper, "I'm just trying to pay attention, read swings, know certain players' tendencies and where people hit the ball."[35]

JBJ was a last-minute addition to the Red Sox roster in 2013— he had hit .441 (26-for-59) in spring training as of the day he was added. Final stats—in 62 at-bats, he hit .414 with 12 RBIs and two home runs.

He was, in Peter Abraham's words, the "star of the camp."[36] And he shone on defense and on the base paths. Veteran outfielder Shane Victorino walked by as a scrum of sportswriters surrounded Bradley looking for quotes after he had made the team. Victorino told JBJ, "They love you now, but they'll be [expletive] burying you within a week."[37]

As the 22-year-old continued to impress, his performance under the Florida sun spawned a heated debate. Was he ready to jump directly to the Red Sox from Double A or would he benefit from further seasoning at Triple-A Pawtucket? Coming off a dispiriting last-place season in 2012, the fans up in the still-chilly north were already salivating at the prospect of seeing the team's top prospects for the 2013 season. And Jackie was not just another hopeful. He was being touted by Red Sox insiders as a once-in-a-lifetime-caliber player. As he was cruising along above the .430 mark he was informed of the interest he was getting in Boston. He seemed surprised and a bit nervous. "I just enjoy playing ball," he told Ron Chimelis of *MassLive.com* in late March. "I hope people don't put a whole lot of expectations on me."[38]

It's easy to see that Jackie didn't yet know much about Boston fans. "I don't really know my chances," he modestly added. "I don't worry about my chances. I sleep well at night." Everyone seemed to have an opinion, pro or con. If he was added to the opening day roster he would be eligible for free agency in 2018; if he was sent to the minors for nine games, that date would be 2019. The always-outspoken Curt Schilling thought he should spend some time in Triple A; Bill James's statistical senses told him he could make the big jump to the majors. Meanwhile, General Manager Ben Cherington and manager John Farrell weren't tipping their hand.

The argument continued to rage in Bradley's head, but he didn't express an opinion to the media. "I just came here trying to improve every day, learn from the veterans, and make a good impression on the new coaching staff," he said.

When the debate had cooled and the Boston weather up north had warmed, he opened the 2013 season with the Red Sox. Jackie Bradley Jr.'s major-league debut came on Opening Day, April 1 in Yankee Stadium. His parents and fiancée were there to take it all in. Bradley played left field and batted eighth in the lineup. Jacoby Ellsbury occupied Jackie's future position in center field and Shane Victorino was in right. Bradley was the youngest Opening Day starting outfielder for the Red Sox since Dwight Evans in 1973. He played LF exclusively during his first stay before being sent down. Only on May 31, after being brought back up, did he first play in center.

When he debuted, he had yet to play a game in Triple A. He hadn't even been on the Red Sox's 40-man roster. Shea Hillenbrand (2001) was the last Red Sox player to make the Opening Day roster out of Double A.

Standing in front of his locker at Yankee Stadium the day before the season began (both teams had a brief workout), Bradley said, "Anything's possible, apparently. I'm ready to start the adventure."

The team was coming off that last-place 2012 season in which they were 69–93, their worst record since 1965.

While Jackie didn't get a base hit, he drew three bases on balls and scored two runs. The first walk, off CC Sabathia, loaded the bases in the top of the second. He moved up one base on a single, another on a groundout, and then scored on Victorino's single between third and short. The run was the third of the inning and proved to be the game-winning run, as the Sox triumphed, 8–2. In the top of the seventh, he earned his first run batted in, on a ball hit back to the pitcher on which Will Middlebrooks scored from third base. Bradley also scored the eighth run of the game, in the top of the ninth. He also made a run-saving catch off a deep drive by Robinson Cano with a runner on second in the fourth inning for the third out.

Following a scheduled off-day, it was Red Sox-Yankees again on April 3 and JBJ got his first big-league base hit. First time up, he was a hit by a pitch and scored the second Red Sox run, in the second inning. The following inning, he hit a two-out single right up the middle off Cody Eppley, scoring Victorino from second, making it 4–0 Red Sox, and then scored the fifth run following a double and a single. The Red Sox won, 7–4. Bradley had scored what ultimately proved the winning run. He drove in another in the third game of the set but Boston lost, 4–2. Despite that, he was only hitting .200.

Driving in one run in each of his first three major-league games impressed people. Going all the way back to 1920, the only Red Sox players to have an RBI in each of their first three games were Jim Rice in 1974 and JBJ in 2013. He scored two runs in both of this first two games. The only other Red Sox player since 1913 to have done so was Sam Horn in 1987.

He started Boston's first six games, but he soon hit a wall and went 14 at-bats without getting the ball out of the infield, striking out six times. He was remarkably sanguine about it, seeming to reflect a deep self-confidence: "I can only get better. It'll all work out. I'm going to keep learning, I'm going to keep fighting, I'm going to keep grinding....The learning curve is always going to be there. I'd rather face adversity now... This is all just an adjustment period. I'll be fine."[39]

Jackie's batting average had slipped to .097 on April 17 when he was asked to go to Triple A and play for the Pawtucket Red Sox.

He wasn't going to be discouraged. The Red Sox knew the kind of personality he had. That was, in large part, because they got to know him even before they signed him. Their scouts put in the effort. Jackie himself said: "I'd say of all the teams I spoke to before I was drafted, the Red Sox did the most work on that side of it. They really tried to get to know me as a person."[40]

Bradley was on the Pawtucket shuttle for much of the season, returning to the Red Sox for games from May 29 to June 5, July 9 to 12, and then (after the International League season ended) from September 7 through the end of the year. For Pawtucket, he appeared in 80 games, batting .275 with 10 homers and 35 RBIs. For Boston, he got into 37 major-league games and hit .189 (.280 on-base percentage) with three homers and 10 RBIs. His first home run had come at Fenway Park on June 4 off the Rangers' Justin Grimm, hit to deep right field—over the visitors bullpen and into the seats.

The year 2013 was a good one for the Red Sox, who finished first in the AL East, then beat the Rays, Tigers, and Cardinals in the three rounds of the postseason, wrapping up each of the rounds one game before what would have been the final game. After beating St. Louis in Game Six of the World Series (and winning their first World Series at home since 1918), the Red Sox were world champions. Bradley had not been on the playoff roster, but he did get his first world championship ring. Shares that year topped $307,000—there were 58 full shares voted.

JBJ showed just enough in 2013 that the Red Sox felt okay about letting go of Jacoby Ellsbury. After signing a $153 million contract with the Yankees, Ellsbury hit .264 in five seasons for New York (he'd hit .297 for the Red Sox) and was unable to play a good percentage of the time, including the entire 2018 season.

Jackie did get a World Series ring in 2013, of course. But, he later said on the brink of the postseason in 2016, "I honestly feel like I didn't earn that one. Obviously, I played on the team, but I didn't feel I contributed. Now I have a chance to really earn one."[41] It was an accomplishment he fully shared with all his teammates in 2018.

After hitting just .189 in those 37 games his first year with the Red Sox, Jackie said in early 2014 that he considered himself blessed to have made the big leagues after only one year in the minors. "I wouldn't like to say I was rushed," he said. "I put myself in that opportunity and tried to compete and have fun. You're learning so much. Just hanging out with the older players and picking their brain a little bit, you learn more about the game . . . You always want to have improvement. You want to get more comfortable with the situation. I was bouncing back and forth and I don't want to get used to that. I got a feel for the majors last season and I feel like I'm going in the right direction."[42]

Except for one stretch with the PawSox from August 18 to 31, JBJ spent the full 2014 season with Boston.

Having lost Ellsbury to free agency, the Sox brought in Grady Sizemore, but he only saw duty in 52 games. Despite coming off a world championship, it was a disappointing season—to say the least. The team finished back in last place. JBJ got in a lot of work, but still came in under the Mendoza Line (at .198). His approach to life served him well. In a preseason story on crying in baseball, he told the *Globe*'s Stan Grossfeld, "I was never really a crier. Every day's a new day. Get back out them and go get 'em tomorrow, it's just a mindset some people have. It's done and over with, time to move on. And use it to your advantage next time."[43]

The Sox had added Yoenis Cespedes, and it looked as though Bradley and Victorino were going to have to jockey for playing time. Victorino, however, had to undergo back surgery. This presented an opening for Bradley, who was struggling offensively at the time.

The Red Sox were patient with him—though to some extent they didn't have a lot of other options. GM Ben Cherington said, "We expected Jackie to be our center fielder of the future back in the winter. We just didn't know what date that was going to start on. I don't think anything's really changed there."[44]

By mid-June, Sizemore was released. Though he had slumped over the first couple of months of the season, from June 19 to July 25 Bradley hit very well—.307 (.358 OBP) over 27 games. Peter Abraham wrote in the *Boston Globe* that it "suggested he had adapted to major league pitching after looking overmatched earlier in the season."[45] But then he hit a 0-for-24 stretch, with 12 strikeouts. Cherington said, "His defense has been elite. We know at some point there has to be a little bit more offense. He knows that, too."[46] One odd note. At the end of June, Jackie said he had started working out in the cage, batting right-handed, maybe to become a switch hitter. He said, "I've been hitting lefty since I was about 8, but I'm a natural righty. I probably have more power righthanded."[47]

The Sox did something unusual on July 9, 2014, in Chicago. Playing the White Sox, they started five rookies in the game—Bradley, Betts, Brock Holt, Bogaerts, and Christian Vázquez. The Elias Sports Bureau said it was the first time they'd done that since April 22, 1952. The youngsters helped the Sox to a 5–4 win.

Just when it seemed that he was on the verge of turning things around offensively, Bradley hit a wall and at one point in August went 35 at-bats without a hit, striking out 17 times. He was sent down to Pawtucket on August 18, and Mookie Betts was brought up from the Rhode Island Triple-A affiliate. Bradley was 0-for-5 that first night against Wilkes-Barre.

When he returned to the Red Sox, he hit another very cold spell, collecting only one base hit in 36 September plate appearances, without even one run scored, and struck out 10 times. He finished the season at .198.

Defensively, it was a very different story. Manager John Farrell said that Jackie Bradley Jr. was the best center fielder in the game. He hadn't committed his first error until September. Meanwhile, Jackie's strong arm from center field had grabbed the attention of teammates and coaches. Prior to a game at Fenway he reversed the regular order of things, throwing a ball from home plate into the center-field stands, much to the delight of observers.

He was not, however, a hot commodity—not someone the Red Sox could even effectively use as trade bait. Boston hadn't had a lot of other choices, though. In 2014, Bradley had more plate appearances than any other outfielder on the team.

Bradley may have the best poker face on the Red Sox. Whether he's 0-for-3 or 3-for-3, his emotions are usually well hidden behind the "resting calm" facade. Whether in the field or at bat, there is little fist-pumping or other outward expressions of joy when he does something that brings Fenway crowds to their feet. It's called poise, or perhaps calm, and it helps him get through a 162-game season of highs and lows.

Jackie may not flash his "Killer B" smile quite as often as Betts, but he still has fun playing the game. Pay attention the next time Bradley catches the final out of an inning. He immediately channels Tom Brady by throwing a lead pass to his close friend and wide receiver Mookie Betts as he runs his route to the dugout. Actually, since he's an LA Rams fan, he probably channels Jared Goff. When Betts corrals the final out, he becomes QB and throws to Bradley John Farrell didn't always exhibit quite as much confidence in Bradley as Bill Belichick does in Tom Brady. "I'm always fearful some fan is going to get it in their nachos and their beer," he once admitted.[48]

For most major-league ballplayers, life on the road can be tedious. For Jackie Bradley Jr., each road trip is a chance to expand his horizons and soak up the cultural and culinary delights of the area. When the Red Sox visit Seattle, for instance, he takes in the Space Needle and Pike's Place Market. But his two favorite cities are Baltimore and Toronto. Baltimore is the nearest park to his home state of Virginia and gives him a chance to reconnect with family and friends. As for Toronto, he says he likes the infrastructure of the city and the people. "It's just a neat town," he says. "The people are friendly. It's a really cool environment."

Maybe it was this openness to new things and his love of discovery that led to his trip to England on behalf of the Red Sox. In December 2018, when the Red Sox chose an ambassador to send to London to promote the June 2019 games against the New York Yankees—the first major-league baseball games ever to be played in Europe—they selected Jackie Bradley Jr. Asked whether he thought the British would become enthused about witnessing baseball firsthand, he said, "I think for the most part cricket is what's on their minds, but, yes, they're excited about seeing the rivalry between the Red Sox and Yankees. And, we're excited to come here, too." He did say, regarding cricket test matches, "I can't imagine playing for five days."[49]

A Tale of Two Cities (2015)

Because he had always hit well at every other level, before he hit the majors, there was still hope he would come around. Maybe having Chili Davis as hitting coach in 2015 would make a difference.

The 2015 season was a tale of two cities for Bradley, specifically Boston and Pawtucket. His playing time was pretty evenly split between the two—74 games in Boston and 71 in Pawtucket. On August 22, 2014, Red Sox GM Ben Cherington signed Cuban ballplayer Rusney Castillo to a shocking seven-year, $72.5 million contract to play with the Boston Red Sox. They brought him to Boston fairly quickly, and in 20 games during September 2014 he played center field for the Red Sox, batting .333 with two homers and six RBIs. It was a decent start. The Sox had obviously invested very, very heavily in Castillo. As Nick Cafardo wrote in the *Globe* right after the signing, "Castillo crowds out Jackie Bradley Jr. and Mookie Betts . . . .The Red Sox have a lot of trade chips now."[50] That said, in January 2015 Peter Abraham wrote that Bradley had been kept in the Red Sox lineup as long as he had, despite his .198 average, because of his "game-changing defensive skills."[51] The team was aware of his quick reaction times that helped him get almost uncanny jumps on balls hit to the outfield; from the day he'd joined the Red Sox he had been part of their neuroscouting program, which was initiated in 2010. "It was part of our routine," Jackie told Alex Speier. "It was a competitive thing because there were rankings. That's what kept it fun. If it wasn't like that, it would have been like homework."[52] He'd spent enough time in the majors in 2014 to qualify for a Gold Glove and was one of the three finalists in center field. His 13 assists tied him for third in the major leagues, and his defense was credited with saving 14 runs.[53] But he finished the 2014 season going 1-for-36.

As it worked out, both Castillo and Bradley started the 2015 season in Pawtucket. Jackie was solid on defense; it was his offense that was the challenge. After striking out 152 times in his first 530 major-league plate appearances, Boston thought he needed more time in the minors. Not using him to start the season also helped the team to maintain pre-arbitration control over him for a longer period of time. But he had a .394 on-base percentage in the minors, so the team thought he just needed more work at the plate to hopefully learn better how to address big-league pitching.

Jackie and his wife Erin honeymooned at Sandals in Antigua and Barbuda and then set up their home in Naples, about 45 minutes from Ft. Myers. Right after the first of the year, he started working with Red Sox assistant hitting coach Victor Rodriguez. "He told me exactly what I needed to hear," said Rodriguez. "Jackie had a plan." His goal was to take quicker, shorter swings. "I felt the same way." The team's hitting coach, Chili Davis, said, "Jackie can hit. Sometimes it takes guys a little longer at the highest level. But Jackie can hit."[54] Shane Victorino was the Red Sox right fielder to start the season, but he was only batting .143 through April 22. Jackie was called up for the game on April 28, but not used, and then sent back to Pawtucket. From the start of the season through May 9, the Sox played Daniel Nava, Allen Craig, and Brock Holt in right field. With a record of 13–17, they decided to make some changes.

On May 10, they optioned Craig to Pawtucket and started Bradley. The plan was to have him bat against righties and Victorino against lefties. He had been hitting .343 for the PawSox when he was called up. After six games without a base hit, he was sent back to Pawtucket, and Castillo was brought up for about a month. Jackie came back to Boston from June 25 to July 2. Batting .133, he was sent back to the PawSox yet again. His third call-up came on July 20 and then he stuck with the team through the end of the season. When Victorino was dealt to the Angels on July 27, Castillo was brought up and also stayed through the end of the year.

The Red Sox outfield never stabilized all season long, one of the reasons they finished in last place in the AL East. Castillo played 48 games in right field, 24 in left field, and six games in center. He appeared in 80 games and hit for an average of .253 with five homers and 29 RBIs.

JBJ played in 74 games and hit for a comparable .249, but more productively. He homered 10 times and drove in 43 runs. He played 32 games in right field, 27 in center, and 17 in left. John Farrell considered Jackie the best defensive center fielder in all of baseball. But he didn't want to displace Mookie Betts from center field unless he was more confident that Jackie would elevate his offense enough to establish himself on the team. Having Jackie play right field, though, was—in the words of one unnamed National League scout—"like playing Brooks Robinson at second base."[55] Sox executive Dave Dombrowski reportedly preferred to see Bradley play center and Betts play in right.[56]

Back with the Sox to close out the season, he seemed to be enjoying himself more. "Let's just say I feel more comfortable," he said. "I'm proud that I never changed as a person. I had to change as a hitter."

There was a stretch, from August 6 to September 7, when he went on a true tear, batting .424 over 28 games. Throughout his first several years, there were streaks when he couldn't get a hit and streaks when he led the team in hitting.

On August 15, Bradley set a Red Sox record and tied a major-league record with five extra-base hits (three doubles and two homers) in one game. He drove in seven runs in the 22–10 win over the visiting Mariners.

As September rolled around, he was looking better and everyone was glad he had stuck with the team.

Heading into the latter half of September, he hit another rough patch, going 1-for-32 with 18 strikeouts. On the 19th, he came up in the ninth inning with the Sox down by two to Toronto. The Red Sox had been 0–65 when trailing after eight innings and the Blue Jays had been 73–0 when leading after eight. With a runner on base and none out, JBJ homered to right field to tie the game. The Sox scored three more runs and won the game. It felt good, he acknowledged. Why had he been struggling so badly? "Kind of sounds weird to say this, but trying to be too perfect."[57]

Fenway to Stay (2016)

It was Jackie Bradley Jr., not Castillo, who had the better future. In 2016, JBJ was with the Red Sox all year long—and became an All-Star. He played 156 games. Only Betts (158) and Bogaerts (157) played more. Castillo played in nine games, with only eight plate appearances. He was 2-for-8 without a run batted in. Even though he had a guaranteed salary through 2020, Castillo has never played in another major-league game. That might have been Bradley's fate, too. Before camp opened in 2016, Nick Cafardo recalled "the hype on Bradley two spring trainings ago, when he looked like the second coming of Willie Mays and it didn't turn out that way."[58]

This was the year that he became cemented into Fenway's center field. In a 2017 interview with WEEI's Rob Bradford, Jackie admitted that he didn't feel like a part of the Red Sox until 2016. The team loved his glove and his arm but had been less than impressed with his offensive contributions. In 2014 he'd batted a paltry .198 and in 2015 he continued to struggle until a late-season surge raised his average to a semi-respectable .249 and gave us a glimpse of what he could do. Still, many people were openly questioning how long the team would wait for him to break out at the plate. The Red Sox were in the embarrassing position of coming off of consecutive last-place finishes in the AL East.

Despite that bad patch in September, he had hit .294 over his final 50 games, though, and in Dave Dombrowski he had a big supporter. The new top baseball man with the Red Sox had tried to trade for Bradley when Dombrowski was with Detroit. He was, wrote the *Globe*'s Christopher Gasper, "a card-carrying JBJ fan." Gasper himself added, "If Hanley Ramirez trying to play the outfield was high comedy, then Bradley tracking down fly balls is performance art."[59] From his debut through the 2015 season, JBJ had played in 232 games, fewer than half the games the team played over those three years, but his 10 double plays were three more than any major-league outfielder during those years.

Bradley himself pointed out that he need only look to teammate David Ortiz to see a player on whom others (the Minnesota

Twins) had bailed, but who ultimately triumphed. "There are going to be people who don't like the way you play the game for your whole career . . . That's where you've got to tell yourself, 'I believe in you.' I don't need anybody to believe in me. I believe in myself. I'm very confident. I know I can play this game at the highest level."

It is impressive how self-confident he was. In late May, looking back on all the times people tried to comfort him when he was struggling in 2014, he said, "I don't like to hear constant encouragement. It gets annoying. I was fine . . . I'm a grown man. I'm not down and out . . . I was tired of hearing words." Some scouts felt he needed a change in scenery. According to Bradley, "I didn't pay attention to any rumors. It really comes down to yourself in the end. You have to want it. You have to have that fight."[60]

In 2016, he showed that he could also hit major-league pitching. He batted .267 with 26 homers and 87 RBIs. And, of course, there was that 29-game hit streak that captured the imagination of the baseball world for the better part of two months. He was selected to the AL All-Star team, the ultimate in acceptance for a big-league ballplayer.

More important than acceptance by baseball, though, was his acceptance as part of the team. "Believe it or not . . . this year was the first year I actually felt I was part of a team," Bradley told Rob Bradford on his *BradfoSho* podcast.[61] He was now the everyday center fielder, which added to his comfort level and allowed him to relax and enjoy the camaraderie of the game.

Based on his regular-season stats, Bradley played at his best to date in 2016. He established personal bests in average (.267), home runs (26), RBIs (87), and runs scored (94). He played right field in the All-Star Game and was 2-for-2, with two singles.

He still showed a streakiness throughout the season, batting .298 with 14 homers and 55 RBIs in the first half of the season, but only .233/12/32 in the second half. Getting just a little more granular, four months exemplified the hot and cold bat Bradley wielded:

May	.381
June	.218
July	.298
August	.198

May was an especially memorable month for Bradley, as he batted .381 with a 1.175 OPS and 8 homers. On June 2, he was announced as the Outstanding Player of the Month. And that wasn't even his most exciting news of the day—his wife Erin gave birth to their first child, Emerson Claire, that day too. In the end, it all added up to a very good season, but the streakiness was a little frustrating at times—great in the months when he was going well, but then to lose over 100 points in the following month left a few scratching their heads.

He did hit considerably better against right-handed pitchers than lefties—23 of his 26 homers came against righties, and he hit for 33 points higher in average.

Why had he been more successful in 2016? Perhaps it was because he was more aggressive at the plate, swinging at pitches earlier in the count. As he was brought up with the Red Sox, he was taught the same philosophy as Sox players of the day were: make the pitcher work. Run up the count. "It works for some people," he said. "It didn't work for me . . . I want to make the pitcher work by getting constant base hits. I'm trying to be a hitter; I'm not trying to work counts. That doesn't work for me."[62]

In April 2016, the Sox outfield—Betts, Bradley, and Brock Holt—began to develop the after-victory routine of bowing to each other and acting out taking a photograph or shooting a film of the one who stood out among them in that game—the win-dance-repeat ritual that captivated fans. But JBJ also started off the "baseball/football pass" that eventually took its place. It could happen at the end of any inning, not necessarily the end of a game. Speaking of Betts, whom he calls "Markus," Bradley said, "I just caught a ball one day and motioned to him and said, 'Go.' He went and I threw it."[63]

The Red Sox finished first in the AL East, four games ahead of the second-place Orioles. They were swept in three Division

Series games by the Cleveland Indians. Jackie was only 1-for-10 in the ALDS, his one hit a single in the bottom of the ninth in Game Three. It was a 4–3 game and he was the potential tying run, but he was left stranded on second base.

Shaky at the Plate, Sensational in the Field (2017)

At spring training in 2017, Jackie Bradley Jr. was sporting a new uniform number. In previous seasons he had worn number 44 briefly, and then 25, a number that many Red Sox fans feel should have been retired years ago in honor of the late Tony Conigliaro. Bradley switched to number 19 for four specific reasons: his birthday is April 19, his mother was in labor for 19 hours before he entered the world, Jackie Robinson was born in 1919, and because his friend and mentor, former center fielder Fred Lynn, wore the number during his time with the Red Sox. Jackie had also donned number 19 during his spectacular college career at the University of South Carolina.

In 2017, the Red Sox sported a fully home-grown outfield. With Benintendi a regular in left field, they had Betts in right and Bradley in center, all three of them drafted by the Red Sox and products of the farm system. Given Bradley's 2013 debut, there was only one member of the 2017 Sox that had been with the team longer than JBJ—Dustin Pedroia.

One of his goals for 2017 was to cut down on his strikeouts. "If I put the ball in play more often, I have a chance." The growing acceptance of Ks as one strives for more HRs didn't sit well with JBJ. "No matter how much the perception has changed, I hate striking out. You're not supposed to feel this way, but I feel embarrassed." He intended to continue to be aggressive. Late in the count, he felt, the pitcher has the advantage. "The cat-and-mouse game is against you."[64]

After a slow start (Jackie strained a right knee ligament in the fourth game he played and was out two weeks; he was batting only .217 at the end of May), he had a very hot June, hitting .353 for the month. That brought him up to .279, but then he wound down slowly, dropping to .264 as of the end of July, .262 at the end of August, and .245 at the end of the season. Oddly, he'd reversed his success against lefties, batting .276 against them but only .235 against righties. Most of the power was still against righties. He did cut his Ks, from 143 in 2016 to 124 in 2017, but his batting average had also dipped.

One place that he remained astonishingly consistent was center field. As spring training began, he said how much he was looking forward to playing between Betts and Benintendi. "A lot of talent, a lot of athleticism out there. Both of those guys are very smart. Communication is the key, as always . . . All of us really take pride in our defense. It's impacting the game now and being looked [at] as getting closer to hitting in terms of value. I love that it's getting the recognition that it is."[65] He spent spring training focused on his footwork, keeping his body in line and concentrating on the steps he took prior to throwing the ball in, striving for better accuracy.[66]

He continued to turn opponents' hits into outs and seemingly sure homers into longer, louder outs. Even balls hit to the furthest reaches of the infamous Fenway triangle were not beyond his reach. In fact, with the possible exception of Neil Grover, famed percussionist with the Boston Pops, he's the best triangle player who ever performed in Boston. Want proof? Ask Tyler Austin, who was the New York DH on August 21, 2017, in another Yankees-Red Sox battle for bragging rights. Austin caught up with a Chris Sale fastball and rocketed it to Fenway's version of Death Valley. Jackie pursued it, pursued it, and pursued it some more and then, when it looked like it would hit off the wall, leaped into the air and brought it down. Sale stared toward Bradley, unsure whether to believe his eyes.

And if you can't talk to Austin, try his former teammate Aaron Judge or the A's Ryan Healey. They were among the many victims of Bradley's thievery in 2017. Better still, talk to innocent bystander Mookie Betts, himself no slouch in the daylight and night game robbery department. Betts has the best sight line in the house for Bradley's heroics. After he watched his teammate throw runner Matt Carpenter out at the plate after a single, he couldn't contain himself. Oh yes, it should be pointed out that Carpenter was on third base at the time. "I get kind of spoiled," Mookie told the media. "I see it all the time. It's just amazing when you sit back and kind of watch what he does. It's like art. He's the best in the league in my eyes, for sure."[67] Keep in mind that Jackie hadn't yet won a Gold Glove.

The Red Sox finished in first place again in 2017. With a 93–69 record, they edged the Yankees by two games. In the Division Series, they ran up against the eventual world champion Houston Astros, but won only Game Three, losing the clinching game again by one run. None of the other three games were close. JBJ hit .200 in the series, but had five runs batted in the four games. The five RBIs tied him with Rafael Devers for the most among Red Sox batters.

In the 8–2 loss in Game Two, Bradley drove in both runs with a single in the second and another in the ninth. In Game Three, which the Sox won, 10–3, the team entered the bottom of the seventh clinging to a 4–3 lead. Hanley Ramirez drove in a pair, Rafael Devers drove in one, and then JBJ homered down the right-field line off Joe Musgrove to drive both of them in, as well as himself. The ball ticked off former Sox player Josh Reddick's glove and into the stands.

Hot Streaks, Cold Streaks

"Hot or cold," "all or nothing," "good field, no hit." These are some of the terms used to describe Jackie Bradley Jr. at the plate.

"Hits from an open stance," said *SoxProspects.com*. "Closes down well on pitch approach to keep himself balanced. Quick and fluid hands. Generates plus bat speed." Even these glowing early scouting reports came with warnings. "Swing has slight upward plane through the hitting zone, but is a little on the long side," they cautioned, adding, "Can struggle with balls on the inner third due to over-extension. Solid bat control. Projects as a solid-average hitter with work needed hitting inside the ball and honing his approach. Tends to look middle-to-inside consistently. Will need to focus on hitting the other way more in the majors. Tends to hook balls on outer third and roll them over. Patient, and displays strong recognition of secondary offerings."[68]

In 2013, *Baseball Prospectus* experts were glowing in their assessment of his fielding but also raised a few flags about his hitting: "Bradley can handle the stick, but he does have some areas to improve upon. The left-handed hitter generates plus bat speed via quick hands, but he runs into some timing issues when he lands on his front too early, and he can be susceptible to offerings on the inner third due to some over-extension in his swing. Bradley does have the hit tool and batting eye to hit .285–.295 with continued adjustments. Don't expect home run power to be a large part of his offensive game—he projects to hit 8–12 round-trippers at his peak, but the outfielder has 'sneaky' power and can muscle up on mistakes."[69]

So far in his major-league career Bradley has been the prototypical streak hitter. At times, he can do no wrong; at other times he can do nothing right. He has put together impressive hit streaks and has racked up equally eye-popping oh-fers, the longest being an 0-for-35 drought in 2014. His longest hit streak was 29 games in 2016 when he bested Wade Boggs's 28-game streak of 1985 and came within five games of Dom DiMaggio's 1949 team record of hitting safely in 34 straight games. During Jackie's amazing run, he batted .408 with 40 hits, eight homers, and 29 RBIs. Boggs credited a steady diet of chicken for his streak; Bradley's was fueled by Ben and Jerry's ice cream.

Some say that Jackie can't hit southpaws, but there is ample evidence to refute that. Manager Alex Cora brushes aside suggestions that Bradley should be platooned against lefties. It isn't blind loyalty that causes him to say that. The former Red Sox utility man sees it as a strategy to force him to stay back on pitches, to stay inside the ball. "Jackie needs the lefties to get his swing back," Cora said. "As a left-handed hitter, I was a platoon guy for part of my career. Sometimes it became very hard for me to hit righties without seeing a lefty."[70] Cora argues that batting against portsiders encourages him to go to the opposite field more often rather than always trying to pull the ball.

Bradley's hitting woes carried over to 2018 and by the All-Star break, he was hitting .210. He'd had just about enough. Like many Red Sox players before him, he consulted with unofficial hitting guru J. D. Martinez, who offered the credibility that comes with being a hitting scholar and a star. Everyone on the team could see he possessed something undefinable in what he brought to hitting—something involving dedication and magic. He already had 29 home runs, a .328 average, 80 RBIs, a slugging percentage of .644, and an OPS of 1.037—at the halfway mark of the season.

Martinez is a student of the arts and science of hitting and he imparted some of that knowledge to Bradley. Based on Martinez's input, Jackie was convinced that dramatic changes in his hitting approach should be considered. Since J. D.'s primary responsibility was his own hitting, he put Jackie in touch with his own hitting coach, Craig Wallenbrock. Red Sox hitting coach Tim Hyers had consulted with Wallenbrock for several years, making the effort a coordinated one.

After the 2018 season, Bradley made two offseason trips to California—one in November and another in January—to work directly with Wallenbrock. Hyers accompanied him on the latter trip and will help him carry out drills and adjustments consistent with the new hitting philosophy.

Changing a swing is no small thing for any hitter, especially when you've been told from an early age not to let anyone change your swing. Countless promising hitters have been damaged by well-intentioned tampering. Though healthy self-confidence is a good thing, living in denial and resistance to change are not. To his credit, Jackie was willing to listen. In a December 2018 interview, the onetime All-Star made a statement that sounded a bit like a confession made under duress: "What I've been taught my whole life is completely wrong. It's scary to say that, but it's wrong. I feel fortunate enough to make it this far doing it wrong."[71]

For a guy like Bradley, whose swing had become almost a part of him, change required a new mindset. He liked his swing, still had confidence in it. After all, it was good enough to get him to the major leagues. Suggestions that he should change it were unsettling, like being told he'd been walking incorrectly all these years. "The adjustments I needed to make were very, very big adjustments," Bradley told the *Boston Globe*'s Peter Abraham at an early February 2019 spring training workout. "That's not the easiest thing to do during the season when you have a game every day. But I felt I had to." The old swing had been good enough for him in high school and in university. It was good enough to get him drafted. It was even good enough to win him that All-Star selection in 2016. But the previous seasons and the prolonged slumps had forced his hand.

From his home in California, Craig Wallenbock provided as much long-distance assistance as possible. Social media helped, as did text messaging, video, and Skype. So did extended phone calls and the offseason face-to-face sessions. Together, they worked on gradually changing his swing with the goal of getting the ball in the air and generating more power. To do this, he had to abandon golden rules that had been drilled into him since his earliest days in baseball. Mantras like be quick with your swing, put the ball in play, and get on top of the ball needed to be downplayed. Now there were new instructions that took precedence. It was tantamount to lopping off three of the Ten Commandments and replacing them, on faith, with others from less venerable sources. But Wallenbrock made it clear that he didn't want to make Bradley into something he was not. He just wanted to make him use his talents to the fullest. "You have to have your own swing," Bradley said. "But when you look at the great players in the game, they all do the same things."

The newly etched commandments included: Hard contact, on a line or in the air. "It's not forcing the ball in the air," explained Bradley. "You're letting the mechanical adjustments and the path you take to get to the ball to get the ball in the air."[72] Somewhere Ted Williams is smiling.

"It was a business decision to invest in myself," Bradley said of the West Coast pilgrimages. "I needed to do it. To grasp the concepts, there's only so much you can do over the telephone. You only get tidbits that way." He added, "To go there physically and do the drills, to make adjustments after each round, it makes all the difference."

That the Red Sox sought out a second and even a third expert opinion on Bradley's chronic hitting malady suggests that they see untapped potential in his bat. Manager Alex Cora was thrilled that he has taken corrective measures, and on his own initiative.

From the 2018 All-Star break onwards, Bradley posted improved, if not jaw-dropping, numbers, batting .269. He improved his OPS to .827.

And in the playoffs, his performance under pressure suggests he had made the new swing his own. His postseason OPS was .835 OPS, as he contributed five extra-base hits and nine walks to the offense. Bradley was named Most Valuable Player of the American League Championship Series after driving in nine runs in five games against Houston.

That speaks to how invested the Sox are in Bradley, who for years has been a topic of trade rumors. "People ask how can we get better. I look at what Jackie has done and I'm excited to see what he will do over a full season," Cora said. "I'm really looking forward to that. I talk about it all the time."

As for JBJ, the difficult adjustment has been made and his confidence in the new approach is growing. "I'm looking forward to being more consistent and sticking with it," Bradley said. "I know what I want to do and how I want to do it."[73]

Hitting coach Tim Hyers was looking forward to 2019, too. Asked about the streakiness in Jackie's past and whether he might have found something in mid-2018 that served him well, Hyers said, "You've got to give Jackie a lot of credit. Jackie did some things. He's ultra-talented in my opinion. He's got by with some body movements because he has such good hand-eye coordination and he's just a phenomenal athlete. The reason you saw the streakiness is because the league pitched to some of those holes. He would make some adjustments, kind of going back and forth with a few things. He had some trouble with his lower half, getting . . . heading in that direction. He had some quick front hip that caused him to come out of the swing, which created a lot of ground balls on his pull side. You have to give him a lot of credit because after about a month and a half he was getting kind of frustrated with what he was doing, his performance. He said, 'OK, we've got to break this down and I've got to make some adjustments.'

"He did it, and you have to give him so much credit. It was so much fun to watch a guy grind through—in the middle of the season, which I don't suggest. It's really very hard to do at the major-league level, but he was like, 'Hey, I'm getting this. I'm not hitting those ground balls anymore.' He made a lot of adjustments to his swing and he was going in the right direction. He couldn't do it all, because it's really tough to do a lot of things in the middle of a season. He just grinded through it, with the help of all of us. Going to the lab, we call it. His drill routine. Get down in the cage and work like mad scientists. It was so much fun because he was just soaking it up and was determined to make a difference in his career.

"This offseason, he's really made another step. Both of us flew out to California and worked with J. D.'s guy. We took stock. We'd film. We'd talk about stuff, working on a few moves. Getting the move that he wants and then going step by step. Get it on video. Watch it. Go do it. Come back and video. Watch it. Get some more in.

"So far in spring training, he is [looking good]. I'm so excited for him. He's one of the guys who I can't wait to . . . He's a smart guy. Putting it all together, I don't think we're going to see a ton of streakiness from now on. I think he's going to be a lot more consistent hitter now. I just can't wait. I'm so pumped up for him."

When it was brought to Tim's attention that, during the 2018 season, Jackie hit .269 in the second half compared to .210 in the first, but he actually had more runs scored and more runs batted in during the first half, Tim's response was classic.

"It's a funny game, isn't it?"

His Glove Is a Many Splendored Thing

According to Statcast™, Jackie Bradley Jr.'s speed is just a bit above average (his sprint time is 27.8 feet per second). So what makes him a Gold Glove fielder? In actuality, it may be as much mental as physical. Writer Joe Posnanski explored the reasons in an August 16, 2018 piece on *MLB.com*.[74]

Not surprisingly, JBJ has among the quickest jumps in baseball. He takes off at the crack of the bat, before he knows the flight path of the ball. He then adjusts his route, while en route. His reads are invariably on the money, allowing him to get to balls that fall beyond the reach of most outfielders. He is a guess fielder. He cheats toward a certain direction, just as guess hitters anticipate a certain pitch. But "guess" is a bit of a misnomer. At the very least, he should be called an "educated guess" fielder. Jackie knows the hitter, he knows the situation, and he knows his pitcher's repertoire and what he's likely to throw in that situation. All this allows him a head start in the general direction of the struck ball and ample time to adjust and hone in on the precise coordinates. Educated guesses.

This is not to downplay his physicality. Bradley has all the skills and instincts that make up for less than blazing speed. As a scouting report from *Baseball Prospectus* in 2013 concluded, he is very "cerebral." They went on to say:

"A natural center fielder, Bradley displays a high level of grace and fluidity when manning his position. His instincts allow him to move with the crack of the bat, giving him above-average-to-better range despite only average speed . . . Bradley hunts down balls in the outfield, making difficult plays look easy and hauling in chances that most outfielders don't. His well-above-average defense is capped off by a plus arm, making him one of the top, if not the top, overall outfield defenders I've seen in the last handful of seasons in the minors."[75]

On some occasions, his skill in getting to fly balls is underappreciated. Case in point:

On August 10, 2018, Baltimore Orioles batter Caleb Joseph

came to the plate in the bottom of the third with runners on first and second. Joseph tore into a Nathan Eovaldi offering and hit it deep to right-center field. In a split-second Bradley was in full stride and full pursuit. According to the analysts at Statcast™ he had to travel 80 feet in 4.2 seconds to get to the ball. He made it despite the fact that Statcast™ put the probability of a major-league outfielder reaching the ball at 6 percent. In Statcast-speak, he got there because of what MLB Senior Database Architect of Stats Tom Tango calls the "reaction-route-burst phases—the reaction to the hit, the beginning of the route, and the burst of speed that he built up." His speed getting to the ball was determined to be 28.6 feet per second. To the surprise of everyone in the ballpark, including the Orioles' play-by-play announcer, he missed the ball and two runs scored. "E8" flashed on the scoreboard. The irony is that JBJ had turned this into a routine play, but in fact it was anything but that. If only 6 percent of outfielders could even have reached it, should it have been called an error?

"It was a miraculous thing," wrote Posnanski. "But Bradley is so good at getting these jumps and was so right at that moment, that he made it look routine." There was no need for a diving attempt or a last-minute lunge. He was there.

The point of this story isn't to show that even great fielders make errors—quite the opposite. It's easy for fans to applaud diving catches or leaping catches to rob a hitter of a homer. Highlight reel plays show great skill and Jackie has had more than his share. This was not a miraculous catch. It was ruled an error, but the fact that he had gotten to it—in time to make it look routine—was miraculous. The fact is that Jackie gets putouts on balls that for others aren't even chances.

Posnanski's conclusion? "We judge how a play looks rather than how the play actually went. Even now, when you show someone the Bradley play, they cannot believe that it was incredible. He made getting there look so easy that it's hard to see the extraordinary skill it took."[76]

It does make you wonder if perhaps JBJ would have a couple more Gold Gloves if these facts were taken into consideration.

Former Red Sox center fielder Fred Lynn knows something about the importance of getting good jumps on a ball. "Jackie and I both got great jumps. We both had great anticipation. Speaking for myself, I know my pitchers on that day and I can see by the way guys are swinging at them if they're going to turn on them or if they're going to hit the ball the other way. So I might cheat the other way when he's on, or I might move back to pull when he doesn't have it or he's missing his spots. Back in the day, because the outfields were so different, and the drainage was awful in some outfields—like Fenway—if it's a real slow track, I might move in because the ball can't get past you in the gaps because it's too wet. So there's all these little things that go into it: the wind, the sun, everything on every pitch is different, especially at Fenway Park. So all these things are going through your head and I'm adjusting pitch by pitch where I'm going and what I'm playing. Same for Jackie.

"They talk about my grace in the outfield. Well, some people say I had grace because I was slow. Jackie is fast and he gets a great jump. I just had long, loping strides, but I covered ground. I ran track and I was fast—a lot faster than people gave me credit for. Not as fast as Jackie but I was a multiple sport guy so when you watched me in center field from the bleachers, I had all the footwork of a basketball player, or a defensive back in football because I did these things. So now it's just instinctual. Having seen many balls off the bat I knew where it was going as soon as it was hit. My routes were really good and my footwork was good. I'll match myself and Jackie with just about anyone I ever saw with getting a jump on the ball."

Another prerequisite for playing center field in ballparks like Fenway is a good arm. Through the years, Boston's middle outfield position has featured rifles such as Lynn and Reggie Smith and a few popguns like Johnny Damon. Jackie Jr. not only has a high-caliber arm but one that is deadly accurate from great distances.

"Bradley's got a good arm," says Lynn. "I've seen him throw runners out while still almost flat-footed. When I used to throw, I almost face-planted a lot of times because I had all my momentum going towards the plate or the base I was throwing to and would almost fall down. JBJ has bigger shoulders than me and a lot of times he just flat-foots his throws over the top. Yeah, he's got a good arm. I can't say that his is better than mine or mine is better than his, but we could both throw accurately, there's no question."

In 2017, Bradley had had a steady year, one without a lot of second-guessing by the Boston media. He'd dipped a bit in offensive production—average as well as power. There was postseason speculation about him being traded, and his name came up often in trade rumors, but it was always brought up by other teams hoping to acquire him. "We like our outfield," Dave Dombrowski said after the GM meetings in November. An anonymous major-league source said, "Dave values defense. I'd be surprised it they moved [Bradley.]"[77]

A Roller Coaster Season (2018)

Many Sox were looking forward to playing for incoming manager Alex Cora in 2018. It was a season free from some of the drama of the preceding years, and also a season in which the Red Sox won a franchise-best 108 regular-season games. That sort of winning makes everyone on a team look good. Jackie had what could be called a disappointing season at the plate. He saw his average dip again, to .234, with his 13 homers half of what they had been in 2016, and his RBI count dipping again, too. Lefties haunted him; he hit just .185 off southpaws. He was .251 against right-handers. This was a year in which he took a long time to get going. He hit under .200 in both April and May and only reached an even .200 as of the end of June. Much stronger months later on—particularly August—helped bump up his average.

Defense was still JBJ's strong card, though. On June 15, *Globe* columnist Nick Cafardo pointed out that Paul Blair's 17-year career batting average was .250. Blair had always been prized by Baltimore for his defense.

Cafardo's colleague Dan Shaughnessy had had a little fun before the season had begun, writing, "[T]he analytics army loves [Bradley] for his defense. Bradley has a career WAR of 10.8. No one really knows what that means, but evidently it's why you don't trade him for a guy who can hit 35–40 homers."[78]

Then there was that golden arm. Bradley's arm is a glorious thing to behold. Picture Zeus hurling lightning bolts but with something extra on them. On June 19, he made an eighth-inning catch in center field against the Twins in Minnesota. The ball traveled 317 feet and settled into Bradley's glove for what everyone in the ballpark assumed was a sac fly that would score a run. To the surprise of everyone, including Red Sox catcher Sandy Leon, Jackie caught the ball with momentum moving plateward and unleashed the mother of all throws. Statcast™ later determined that it was moving at a rate of 103.4 mph. Leon took the throw and applied the tag to a shell-shocked Robbie Grossman for the out. The Red Sox lost the game, 6–2, but fans were still buzzing about the laser-like throw as they filed out of Target Field. After the game, manager Alex Cora described the play for reporters. "I saw him getting an angle, and I was like, 'This might be fun here.' It's kind of like showcase baseball. 'The scouts are looking, and I'm going to throw it as hard as I can to see if I can get him, and I did.' That was a great play."

True to form as the ultimate team player, Bradley was subdued after the eye-popping play. He was still dwelling on the run-scoring error he had made on a double by Eduardo Escobar in that same inning. When asked to describe his jaw-dropping throw, his reply was curt. "Just got behind the ball and made a throw," said Bradley. "I don't care about the throw."[79]

At year's end, he did have a .314 on-base percentage, and had added 18 runs scored more than his 2017 total. And his defense was solid—impressing the voters enough to win him his first Gold Glove, thanks to his superb fielding in center. His over-the-shoulder running catch on May 28 robbing Toronto's Kendrys Morales of what seemed like a sure extra-base hit to the triangle prompted both Andrew Benintendi and David Price to marvel. "He knows every inch of that outfield, and how much room he has," Benny said. "He makes those kind of plays all the time . . . He covered something like 116–117 feet or something like that. That's crazy." Price, acknowledging the struggles Bradley had been having all season at the plate, said, "We all know how much he cares, how hard he works—in the weight room, in the video room, in BP, in the cage. To kind of see somebody struggle like that, you feel for them . . . He never lets it affect his defense and that's what the really good players do. He continues to make web gem after web gem and that's why we love Jack."[80]

Alex Cora was certainly appreciative of Bradley's game, as was longtime *Boston Globe* columnist Bob Ryan, who said he'd seen every Red Sox center fielder since 1964 and it wasn't even close—Bradley was the best.[81] Bradley was also far more active on the basepaths, stealing 17 bases, which matched the total of the two previous years added together. He was caught just once. The 94.4 percent success rate was the best in the majors for all who attempted at least 15 steals.

That Gold Glove he finally secured in 2018 was perhaps overdue, but certainly well-deserved.

Jackie has taken part in 17 double plays, 15 from center field and one each from left and right. The 17 DPs ranks him first among all major-league outfielders over the past five seasons. Eight of the double plays came in 2014 alone; apparently word got around. No other outfielder in the majors took part in more than three double plays that year.

He has 41 assists as a center fielder over the same period of time, third among major leaguers. His 13 assists from CF in 2016 topped the majors.

His nine assists from CF in 2018 tied him for tops in the AL.

Even though he won a Gold Glove in 2018, the standards he set for himself were higher yet. In February 2019, he told reporters in Fort Myers that he felt 2018 was his worst season in the field. (It could be that he had in mind the six errors with which he was charged. In no other year had he had more than the four he had in 2017.)

Anyone who ever played baseball as a kid remembers a favorite glove. It had its own special feel, its own distinctive smell. Many of us slept with that glove the first night we had it. We spent hours oiling it and placing a baseball in the pocket and tying it together tightly with twine overnight. As it got older it acquired character, like a fine wine. Soon it was broken in perfectly, customized to your hand and only your hand, the pocket deep and secure. And then, after a few years had passed, that old glove started to let you down every once in a while. Maybe the webbing broke when you were flagging down a hard-hit liner at first. You repaired it, of course, but then other things started to happen. You could no longer make out the Rocky Colavito signature at the heel, and the rawhide lacing was rotting. Finally, it became so loose and shapeless that it began to resemble a dishrag. It was time for a new glove. The old one was relegated to a place of honor on your dresser until your mother eventually threw it out while you were away at college. If that story sounds personal it's because it is, but it's also universal.

Even a professional like Jackie Bradley Jr. has an attachment to his glove. After all, for him it's also a meal ticket. During spring training, 2019, the time had come for JBJ to retire his old glove. Chad Jennings of *The Athletic* was there in Fort Myers, Florida, to witness it.

Jackie's glove was adorned with JBJ initials in red stitches. "(That) one is no longer a gamer," Bradley told Jennings. "It's retired after it won a Gold Glove. It won a Gold Glove, so it can be sat down now." It's not as if Bradley Jr. ran right out to Walmart to buy a new one. He already had one waiting like an eager minor leaguer for its big moment in the sun. He'd been carefully grooming it for two years in pregame workouts and practice sessions. It was now deemed ready for primetime. "This is the up-and-comer," he announced. His retired glove had served him well for four years.

The Green Monster scoreboard tells the story as Andrew Benintendi catches a fly ball at the warning track in Fenway's left field.
(Adam Glanzman / Stringer)

Exhibiting total concentration, Benintendi is set to unleash his classic swing.
(Maddie Meyer / Staff)

Jackie Bradley Jr. receives congratulations from teammates after scoring against the Atlanta Braves in an interleague game at Fenway in 2018. (Adam Glanzman / Stringer)

A young Bradley demonstrates how he built his reputation as the best center fielder in baseball. This photo was taken in 2014, before he switched his number to 19.
(Jared Wickerham / Staff)

A fresh-faced Mookie Betts runs onto the field before the game against the New York Yankees at Yankee Stadium on June 28, 2014. The following day he made his major league debut and collected his first hit. (Rich Schultz / Stringer)

Mookie uses his full extension to stab the ball before tumbling over the outfield wall at Fenway. (Jim Rogash / Stringer)

Brock Holt greets Jackie Bradley Jr. after JBJ's 8th inning grand slam homer in Game Three of the ALCS at Minute Maid Park in Houston, October 16, 2018. (Bob Levey / Stringer)

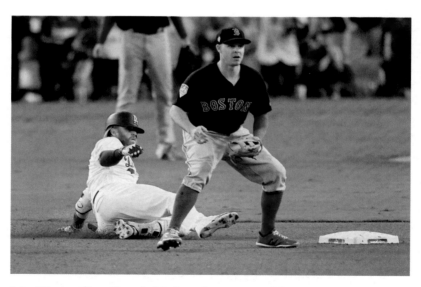

Mr. Versatility, Brock Holt, plays second base in Game Three of the 2018 World Series at Dodger Stadium in LA. (Kevork Djansezian / Stringer)

Brock, Betts, and Benny bust some moves after a 6–3 win over the Arizona Diamondbacks in 2016. (Rich Gagnon / Stringer)

Benintendi and Bradley "video" the footwork of teammate Mookie Betts after a 5–1 win over Toronto on July 19, 2017. (Maddie Meyer / Staff)

The entire hive of Bs celebrate an 8–2 win over the Houston
Astros in Game Three of the ALCS at Minute Maid in Houston.
(Elsa / Staff)

Benny and JBJ compare notes during a break in the action in a September 13, 2018 game with the Toronto Blue Jays. (Maddie Meyer / Staff)

Mookie and Benny head for the warmth of the clubhouse after a cold early April victory over the Tampa Bay Rays in 2018. (Omar Rawlings / Stringer)

Right: With laser-like focus and muscles tensed, smooth-swinging Fred Lynn prepares to attack a pitch. (Hulton Archive / Staff)

Left: Dwight Evans follows the flight of the ball as he heads for first base. (Rick Stewart / Stringer)

The Boston Strongman, Jim Rice, shows the raw power that made him one of the most feared hitters of the '70s and '80s. (Rick Stewart / Stringer)

Photos courtesy of *Getty Images*.

But the new one would be taking early retirement in about two short months. Why?

He had received a shiny, black Rawlings model, still nestled in its box. This one had an added adornment that you can't buy at Walmart—or anywhere else: a beautiful gold patch on the back strap, designating the user as a Gold Glove winner. And yes, even a Gold Glover's gold glove needs to be broken in. "I do like it formed a certain way," he said. "I can't let anybody use it until I completely formed it in where I know the glove will not [bend] anywhere else. So, I'll form it, and then someone can use it because I know it can't be reformed again." He added, 'I'll try to speed up the process."[82]

Fittingly, his now-retired glove was passed along to another Gold Glove Red Sox outfielder. Spring training instructor Dwight Evans—owner of eight Gold Gloves—happened to be without a broken-in glove. Gold Glovers obviously stick together and JBJ bequeathed the worthy relic to Evans. It was fitting because Evans had worked extensively with Bradley on fielding in the minors. They hit it off immediately. "I heard you had a good arm," said JBJ when they first met, which is roughly equivalent to telling Pavarotti that he had a decent voice. But it was his follow-up line that captivated Evans. "He goes, 'I just want you to know, I have a pretty good arm, too.' I loved that!" Evans said. The two have been brothers-in-arms ever since, comparing notes and swapping stories.

Evans is clearly a fan. "If you watch him, watch how he takes fly balls in the outfield during batting practice," Evans said. "It's [like a] game situation. He does that for about 12, 15 minutes. I used to take 12 to 15 of them, and guys will take 8 to 10 of them normally. He goes that whole 12 to 15 minutes and gets after it. I'm so glad. He deserved that Gold Glove."

But even Jackie Bradley Jr. can't play center field with his real Gold Glove, the one fashioned from the precious yellow metal. That's why he turns his attention back to the shiny new leather one at his side. "I may want to just look at it while it's still new," he told Jennings.

Postseason Hitting Redemption

Bradley got to play in 14 postseason games for the Red Sox in 2018, doubling his career total. He didn't hit for a high average, but the hits he did get were usually timely. He was the MVP of the American League Championship Series against the defending world-champion Astros.

In the four postseason games against the Yankees, he only got two hits and never drove in a run, even during the 16–1 shellacking the Sox gave the Yanks in Game Three. But in the ALCS against the Astros, he produced big-time.

With the Sox down, 4–2, in Game Two, JBJ hit a three-run triple off Gerrit Cole in the bottom of the third to give the Sox a 5–4 lead, which they built on to win the game, 7–5. Two nights later, after the series had shifted to Houston, the Red Sox held a one-run lead (3–2) through the first seven innings. In the top of the eighth, the Red Sox loaded the bases off Roberto Osuna and then got an insurance run when Mitch Moreland got hit by a pitch. On a 1-1 count, Bradley hit a grand slam deep into the right-field stands to put the game away. He'd been 1-for-17 with the bases loaded during the regular season. Dan Shaughnessy summed it up: "This was a statement game and Jackie Bradley Jr. made the loudest noise."[83] Shaughnessy had dubbed him a "Coke and hot dog hitter" during the season, meaning when he came to bat, you could get up and get a drink and a hot dog.

The very next night, Jackie drove in two more runs via a two-run homer down the right-field line in the top of the sixth that converted a 5–4 deficit to a 6–5 Red Sox lead. In the 2018 ALCS, he reached base in all five games (two of the times via walks). In the three games in which he got a hit, each of his hits was for extra bases, each drove in multiple runs, and each came with two outs. It's not difficult to see why he was named the Most Valuable Player of the ALCS.

During the season, the coaches and assistants working with Bradley had assured him that "his traditional statistics did not reflect who he was . . . that Bradley's consistent work behind the scenes and approach in the box would culminate in a reversal of fortune." Bradley said they told him, "At the end of the year, you'll do something special. They were right."[84] Red Sox hitting coach Tim Hyers said the same thing. "There was one month when he was third in baseball for hard-hit percentage. It went all through Twitter and on *Red Sox Stats*, a little website. He was like third in baseball for hard-hit percentage and he really didn't get the results. I remember the Houston series, in Houston. I was like, 'Man, you're so unlucky.' He was crushing balls—at people. Goody [Tom Goodwin], our first-base coach, he was so funny. He said, 'Hey, Jackie. Just hang in there, man. Your luck's so bad, you're going to get all your luck in the playoffs. You're going to be MVP of the World Series. All that luck's going to end up in the World Series. Every ball you hit hard's going to fall, in the World Series. You're going to be our MVP.'

"Just joking around, but we said that every time he hit some balls hard and get out, Good would say, 'Hey, Jackie, don't worry about it. They're going to fall in in the World Series or playoffs. You're our MVP.'

"We were one off."

In the five games of the World Series against the Los Angeles Dodgers, Jackie was 3-for-13 (.231), more or less back on par with his regular-season average, but in Game Three, he hit a solo home run that was the first run of the game for the Red Sox. To that point, they had been held scoreless. The Sox rode the 1–1 tie into the 13th inning. They scored once but then gave up a run in the bottom of the 13th. The Sox lost the game in 18, but won the next two games and became world champions for the fourth time in 15 years. Jackie Bradley Jr. had earned himself a ring.

After 16 years as the coach of the Gamecocks, Ray Tanner has become Athletic Director at the University of South Carolina. In early 2019, we asked Jackie's college coach if he continued to follow him. He does. He follows the Red Sox. So, too, do a number of his friends.

"He continued to grow as a player," Tanner said. "It was steady.

Level. When you watch him play—and people tell me all the time, 'Hey, did you see Jackie last night? Did you see the play he made?' I'm going, 'That play was routine. To Jackie.' It might not be routine to a lot of people. But it was routine to Jackie. If you asked Jackie, he expected to make that play.

"That's the thing that stands out to me—just the way he approached the game. He's been a little bit hold and cold offensively, but his glove was always the same. He stays in the mode that 'I've got to take hits away. I've got to make plays.'"[85]

Junior wasn't the only former University of Carolina player to stand out for the Red Sox in 2018. In fact, the postseason turned into something of a Carolina alumni celebration. Former Gamecock Steve Pearce, acquired from Toronto, exceeded all expectations at the plate and when called upon to play first base. After Bradley homered twice—one a grand slam—and collected nine RBIs to win the ALCS MVP award, Pearce went 4-for-12 at the plate and drove in eight runs to win MVP honors in the 2018 World Series. Two Gamecocks, two MVP awards. Carolina's athletic director and former baseball coach wasn't surprised at the duo's contributions to the world championship team. "They're never too high, they're never too low," Tanner told *The State*. "The theme for Boston [this season] was, 'we're a bunch of guys that get along well, and we have a selfless clubhouse.' You have two guys in our former Gamecocks who epitomize that."[86]

Game-Winning Hits by Jackie Bradley Jr.

Jackie Bradley Jr. was the first of the Killer B's to make the majors in 2013, and he was the first to have a game-winning hit. He'd had a couple of big games earlier in the season—his 3-for-5 day at Yankee Stadium on June 1, and his three RBIs (built around a two-run homer) on June 4.

Through the 2018 season, JBJ has 28 game-winning hits. There were plenty of games in which he kicked off the scoring, or helped add a run or two early on. There were times he helped the Sox come from behind and tie up a game. There were times he added insurance runs, in games where Boston already had the lead—like the two-run homer off Ivan Nova in the top of the seventh at Yankee Stadium on September 28, 2015. That turned a 2–1 Red Sox lead into a more comfortable 4–1 margin. The final score was 5–1. There are times he was on base and scored the winning run. The hits listed here, though, are the game-winners, hits that gave the Red Sox the run or runs that were sufficient to win the game.

His first game-winning hit came on Sunday afternoon, September 22, 2013. The Sox had an eight-game lead over the second-place Rays in the AL East and were hosting the last-place Blue Jays at Fenway. The Blue Jays took a 1–0 lead in the top of the second, but after Boston put one across to tie the game in the bottom of the second, JBJ came up with two outs and runners on first and third. Facing Toronto's R. A. Dickey, winner of the 2012 National League Cy Young Award, Bradley took the first pitch and then slammed the second one he saw into deep right field for a three-run homer, giving Boston a 4–1 lead. The game's final score was Boston 5, Toronto 2.

Jackie kicked off 2014 with a spree of sorts—collecting five game-winning hits over a 25-game stretch, and added a sixth in August.

April 3, 2014: A night game in Baltimore, the third game of the young season. The Red Sox had a 3–2 lead after four innings. Neither team scored in the fifth. In the top of the sixth, there were two outs and Will Middlebrooks on second base. Bradley singled to center, driving in Middlebrooks and giving Boston a 4–2 lead. The Orioles scored once in the bottom of the sixth, making it 4–3, but that was the end of the scoring in the game. JBJ's single made the difference.

April 7, 2014: Just three games later, the Sox were home and hosting the Texas Rangers. In the bottom of the second, Bradley singled in Xander Bogaerts to give Boston a 1–0 lead. The Rangers' Mitch Moreland tied it up in the top of the fourth. In the bottom of the fourth, Bogaerts grounded out to lead off the inning, but then two singles followed. With runners on first and third, JBJ hit a grounder into left field, and the Red Sox took a 2–1 lead. They won the game, 5–1.

April 16, 2014: The Red Sox were on the road, playing at U.S. Cellular Field (that was the home of the other Sox, in Chicago). Boston scored in the first, but so did the White Sox, who took a 3–1 lead in the sixth. The Red Sox scored once in the eighth and once in the ninth and the game went into extra innings. Both teams scored once in the 11th. The first two Boston batters in the top of the 14th made outs. The next two drew walks. JBJ was 0-for-5 in the game to that point. He doubled down the right-field line and drove in both baserunners, sending Boston to a 6–4 victory.

April 29, 2014: The Rays were at Fenway for the last game of April. The score was 1–1 after 5 ½ innings. In the bottom of the sixth, A. J. Pierzynski singled in one run to make it 2–1, Middlebrooks doubled to make it 3–1, and then Jackie Bradley Jr. doubled to center field, scoring them both. He'd made it 5–1. The Rays scored three more times, and the Red Sox scored twice more, but it was the fifth run that made the difference in the 7–4 win.

May 2, 2014: He'd had four game-winners in April alone, but quickly added another one on May 2, when the Oakland A's came to town. After the Sox scored once in the bottom of the second, with a runner on first and two outs, Bradley doubled so deeply to center field that even that baserunner—the hardly-fleet Pierzynski—scored all the way from first base and gave the Red Sox the run that won the game in an eventual 7–1 decision.

August 14, 2014: He had one more game-winner in 2014, on Tuesday night, August 14. The Houston Astros were visiting Boston. After 5 ½ innings, the Astros held a 4–1 lead. Scott Feldman seemed to be cruising. Then came the bottom of the sixth. Brock Holt doubled, Dustin Pedroia singled, and David Ortiz singled in Holt. With one out, Mike Napoli singled in Pedroia. Daniel Nava walked, loading the bases, and Will Middlebrooks added an RBI single to tie the game. Feldman departed, replaced by Darin Downs. On six pitches, Bradley drew a bases-loaded walk, giving Boston a 5–4 lead they maintained, and built on, winning, 9–4.

August 9, 2015: There was almost a year between game-winners for JBJ, but he went on a bit of a tear in August and September, and racked up four more. The Red Sox won the Sunday afternoon game in Detroit, 7–2, and Jackie Bradley Jr. had a very big day, with five RBIs. It was his solo home run leading off the seventh inning that provided Boston's third run of the game. His bases-loaded walk in the second inning gave the Red Sox their first run. And his bases-loaded triple in the top of the eighth gave him three more RBIs—insurance runs, for sure.

Five runs batted in was a lot, but Jackie topped that on August 15, with a seven-RBI game. Despite all those runs—a career-high through 2018—none of them represented the game-winner. The Red Sox as a team scored 22 runs and beat the Mariners, 22–10.

August 19, 2015: The fifth run was the one that made the ultimate difference in the Red Sox' 6–4 win over the visiting Cleveland Indians. In the bottom of the fourth, the Red Sox had a 2–0 lead. Then Bradley, facing Corey Kluber, hit a three-run homer over the Green Monster and the Red Sox took a 5–0 lead. As the final score indicates, the team needed every one of those three runs.

September 6, 2015: The Phillies were at Fenway for a Sunday afternoon game, when the Red Sox quickly built a 6–0 lead. It came about after they scored twice in the first inning and four more times in the second. The Phillies scored two runs, one in the third and one in the ninth. The third Red Sox run was the one that won the game. Rusney Castillo led off the second with a double, but was then caught trying to steal third. A single and a walk put runners on first and second. Bradley then tripled down the line in right field and drove both runners in. Those were the third and fourth runs for the Red Sox. The Phillies scored twice, and no more.

September 20, 2015: It was 3–3 in Toronto. The Blue Jays were in first place and the Red Sox were in last place. There were 14 games left on the schedule, and the Red Sox were 14½ games down in the standings. The Jays held a 3–0 lead after two innings. The Red Sox got one in the fourth and two more in the fifth. The game was tied. It remained tied in the sixth and seventh, with neither team scoring. In the top of the eighth, Pablo Sandoval reached first base for Boston on an error by the pitcher. A groundout moved him to second. A single moved him to third. And JBJ hit a sacrifice fly to left-center to score Sandoval and give the Red Sox a 4–3 lead and final score.

April 13, 2016: The Red Sox won 93 games in 2016 and finished in first place. Jackie Bradley Jr.'s base hits won nine of those games. On the night of the 13th, both the Orioles and Red Sox scored two runs in the third inning. Brock Holt walked in the bottom of the fourth and Bradley tripled him home. He scored himself on a slow ground ball, but it was the third run that won the game.

April 24, 2016: Playing the Astros in Houston, JBJ drove in the fifth run for a 5–3 lead, but the Astros tied the game in the ninth. In the top of the 11th, back-to-back singles, a sacrifice, and a walk loaded the bases with one out. Bradley singled, driving in the first of the two runs the Red Sox scored. They won, 7–5.

April 25, 2016: Julio Teheran vs. Rick Porcello at Turner Field. Neither the Braves nor the Red Sox scored a run through six. In the top of the seventh, JBJ hit a solo home run to right field. Neither the Braves nor the Red Sox scored any other runs in the game in the 1–0 Sox victory.

May 30, 2016: On May 6, he had six RBIs in a Red Sox win and on May 9, he had six RBIs in another Red Sox win. In neither game did he have the game-winning hit, but he did on May 30 with a leadoff home run in the top of the sixth in Baltimore. His homer gave the Sox the lead, one they never relinquished in their 7–2 win.

June 28, 2016: Travis Shaw had five RBIs in the 8–2 Red Sox win at Tropicana Field. It was the third run that won the game. In the top of the fifth, Dustin Pedroia walked but David Ortiz grounded into a double play. Hanley Ramirez walked, and Jackie Bradley Jr. doubled down the right-field line, making it 3–2, Red Sox—after which they added five insurance runs.

August 15, 2016: An unusual Monday afternoon game in Cleveland saw the Indians score once in the fourth and add one more run in the eighth. The Red Sox put up a three in the top of the sixth, on a two-run homer by David Ortiz and a solo homer (the difference-maker) by Jackie Bradley Jr.

August 17, 2016: Both teams scored in the second, and the Sox scored twice in the third. With two outs, Mookie walked and JBJ hit a two-run homer to center field off Baltimore's Dylan Bundy. The Red Sox kept adding runs, then the rains came, and it was called after 6 ½, with Boston winning at Camden Yards, 8–1.

August 19, 2016: Every other day, JBJ won a game—the 15th, 17th, and now the 19th. Each game was in another city. On this night in Detroit, the Red Sox scored enough runs in the top of the first to win the game (it was a 10–2 final, helping Rick Porcello improve his record to 17–3). Both Ortiz and Bradley hit two-run homers.

September 6, 2016: The first scoring in the game was Bradley's two-run homer to deep right field, scoring Sandy Leon before him. Chris Young homered right after him. The Red Sox defeated the Padres at Petco Park, 5–1.

May 30, 2017: It was 7–6, Red Sox, on the South Side of Chicago at the catchily-named Guaranteed Rate Field. Four innings were in the books. JBJ worked the count and, on the sixth pitch he saw, hit a ball out, and the Sox added runs eight, nine, and ten. They later added three more, while the White Sox just added one.

June 9, 2017: Friday night at Fenway, and the Tigers were in town. With two runs scored in the first inning and another in the top of the fourth, Detroit held a 3–0 lead. Mitch Moreland homered and Bradley singled in Benintendi in the bottom of the fourth, to draw within one. So it stood until the bottom of the eighth. Moreland singled in Bogaerts to tie the game, and then Bradley homered to give the Red Sox a two-run lead. Craig Kimbrel closed the door.

July 1, 2017: Top of the first in Toronto. Baserunners on second and third, two outs. JBJ swung at Francisco Liriano's first pitch and doubled to left field, driving in both. During the course of the game, the Red Sox added five runs, but Chris Sale allowed no runs at all through seven. They got one in the bottom of the ninth, but they got no more. JBJ's double was the game-winner.

August 20, 2017: The two early runs JBJ drove in this Sunday also won a game. He tripled in the bottom of the second inning, driving in Xander Bogaerts and Sandy Leon. The Yankees got a run in the fifth, but the Red Sox won, 5–1.

September 8, 2017: It was another Friday night at Fenway. The Red Sox scored thrice in the bottom of the first, thanks to a three-run homer by Mookie Betts. They built on that in the fourth. Rafael Devers doubled and Christian Vázquez singled, moving Devers to third. JBJ singled off Tampa Bay's Chris Archer and made it 4–0. By the time the fourth was in the books, Archer was gone and the Red Sox held an 8–0 lead. The Rays did get back three, but it was JBJ's single in the fourth that was the game-winner.

May 29, 2018: It was nearly June before Bradley had his first game-winner of 2018. Before the year was over, though, he had eight. The Red Sox had a 3–1 lead over the Blue Jays. In the bottom of the fourth, Brock Holt hit a one-out single and then stole second. He moved up to this base on a groundout and scored with ease when JBJ singled to left-center field. The 4–1 lead built to an 8–3 victory at game's end.

June 26, 2018: The visiting Angels only scored a lone third-inning run off David Price and three relievers. Leadoff batter Mookie Betts homered in the bottom of the first. Whoever drove in the second Red Sox run was the game-winner, and that honor went once again to Jackie Bradley Jr. His double to shallow left field drove in Devers and Eduardo Nuñez. The Sox scored in every inning but the fourth and eighth and won, 9–1.

June 28, 2018: Hector Velasquez might not have believed his good fortune. Brian Johnson started for the Red Sox and pitched well. It was just his second start of the year, so the Sox didn't want to tax him. He left after four innings, down 1–0 to the Angels. Velasquez came in, saw Devers tie it with a leadoff home run in the bottom of the fifth, saw Holt knock in another run in the sixth, and then watched JBJ hit a two-run homer in the seventh, enough to see Velasquez go to 6–0 on the season.

July 4, 2018: The Red Sox went to the nation's capital for the Fourth of July. Eduardo Rodriguez won the game, with six scoreless innings, backed by a bullpen that threw three more. The Nationals threw out six pitchers. The first three held Boston scoreless for six innings, but in the top of the seventh, Jackie Bradley Jr. hit a one-out double to right-center, driving in Nuñez. The final score was 3–0.

July 15, 2018: It was another Brian Johnson start, but once more he left the game before he would have qualified for a win— this time exiting just one out beforehand. Sandy Leon doubled to lead off the bottom of the fifth, and Bradley doubled, too, to drive Sandy home. It had been a 2–2 tie to that point, and the Red Sox ultimately prevailed, 5–2.

August 2, 2018: Always good to beat the Yankees. Brian Johnson, once more, got the start, but this time he got bombed for three runs in the first inning on a Didi Gregorius home run. He gave up another run in the top of the second when Aaron Hicks homered. Betts drew a base on balls and thus brought in one run for the Red Sox in the second and Steve Pearce homered to lead off the third. In the fourth, Pearce hit a three-run homer, but the Sox didn't stop there. By the time the inning was over, they had scored eight times. JBJ's double drove in their ninth run of the game. Benintendi drove in Bradley to make it 10–4. Gregorius homered off Johnson to lead off the fifth, but Johnson finished the frame and qualified for the 15–7 win (marked by a third Pearce home run.)

August 30, 2018: Back in Chicago to face the White Sox, Rick Porcello gave up four runs in the first two innings. He was gone, but it was still 4–0 White Sox after six innings. In the top of the seventh, Blake Swihart singled in one run, JBJ hit a sacrifice fly for another, and then Betts hit a two-run homer to tie the game. In the top of the ninth, Bradley broke the tie with a single, scoring Ian Kinsler. Benintendi drove in another run, and then J. D. Martinez put down the hammer with a three-run homer.

September 1, 2018: The White Sox won the August 31 game, 6–1, and then the same two teams faced off once more. Boston turned the table, winning this game by the same 6–1 score. Neither team scored for the first four innings. Eduardo Nuñez doubled off the wall in left-center—or so it seemed until the umpires reviewed the call and awarded him a home run, making it 1–0, Red Sox. After two outs, Jackie Bradley came up and hit another homer, this one a no-doubter to deep right field. That was the one that won the game.

So there they are, the 28 game-winning hits off the bat of Jackie Bradley Jr. To date, he's played in 21 postseason games, but hasn't collected a game-winner in any of them, although he has certainly contributed. As noted, he was even the MVP of the 2018 ALCS against the Houston Astros, with nine RBIs in the five games. Overall, he's had 15 RBIs in those 21 postseason games, and in 40 fielding opportunities he's made a couple of spectacular plays and has never committed an error.

Mookie Betts, Right Field

From the time Diana Collins formed a team just to give her five-year-old son a chance to play, Mookie Betts has performed as if the very game of baseball was created just for him. He can do it all and do it with style and a smile. In fact, the only thing that might exceed his winning attitude on the field is his winning personality off it.

Markus Lynn Betts was born in Nashville, Tennessee, on October 7, 1992. His mother finished her weekly league bowling session at 9:30 that evening and went into labor an hour and a half later. Mookie's father, Willie Mark Betts, inspired his first name and Lynn is his mother's middle name. Diana admits that the order of the names was not entirely random. She had assumed her son would be an athlete when he was still in the womb and once she realized that the names they were considering also represented Major League Baseball, she knew she was onto something. "I figured we should just go with it and see how it goes," she said. Did the initials MLB predetermine his occupation? Who knows, but it would be hard to imagine a player who better represents the grand old game.

The nickname "Mookie" also had a sports connection. His parents loved basketball and enjoyed watching Mookie Blaylock, a former NBA guard with their beloved Atlanta Hawks (he also played for the New Jersey Nets and Golden State Warriors). They decided it would be the perfect nickname for Markus and would keep the MLB sequence intact.

Mookie's uncle is Terry Shumpert, former major-league jour-neyman second baseman and outfielder who appeared in 854 games over 14 seasons with the KC Royals, Boston Red Sox, Chicago Cubs, San Diego Padres, Colorado Rockies, LA Dodgers, and Tampa Bay Devil Rays. With the Red Sox in 1995, he hit .252 (.315 OBP) and his career numbers included 49 homers and 223 RBIs. His last year in professional baseball was the 2004 season he spent playing second base (and a few games at shortstop) with the Nashville Sounds. Playing in Mookie's hometown, Shumpert brought him into the clubhouse a lot that year. "He was in the locker room after batting practice, see how the guys act, see how the guys work. He was old enough to be able to pick it up and see how those guys and myself come to work every day and prepare." Shumpert added, "I was able to teach him and talk to him about some of the pitfalls that I believe were obstacles to my career."[87]

Mookie Betts is a superhero now, but one with a few twists. Like Superman or Spiderman or perhaps a combination of the two, he performs heroic deeds only after changing from street clothes into a flashy uniform. Unlike Superman and his alter ego Clark Kent, the action hero Mookie remains mild-mannered and incon-spicuous when he emerges from the dugout to perform amazing feats for his adoring public. Oh, there's no doubt that he can fly, or that he's faster than a speeding fastball. Or that, like Spidey, he can scale walls with ease and capture things in his web.

Physically, Mookie Betts is a man of average stature. The muscles of his 5-foot-9, now 180-pound body don't strain against his jersey, which in any case is loose-fitting, making him appear even less imposing than he is. His powers come from within, not from the outer reaches of the galaxy. As origin stories go, his seems pretty bland. Maybe that's why everyone loves him, because he looks so ordinary, like most of us. We can identify with him. His alter ego and his ego are one and the same.

Even by baseball standards, he doesn't fit the mold of the twenty-first century superstar athlete. Mike Trout, Giancarlo Stanton, and Aaron Judge are more representative of the new generation of ballplayers—tall and muscular with large upper bodies, their appearance openly announcing their power to everyone in the ballpark. Approaching the plate, Mookie looks underwhelming. There is no flourish, no flexing, no looming presence. His walk to the plate borders on the nonchalant, and his demeanor is mild and reserved. When the umpire or opposing catcher greets him, his smile becomes his most noticeable feature. It's a great smile, a genuine smile.

Only when he digs in and stares out to the mound do you begin to see subtle changes in his body language. His elfish smile morphs into an Elvis sneer, the right side of his mouth curling upward as if he's about to belt out an impromptu version of "Jailhouse Rock." In fact, his focus is complete, his mind is working overtime. It is a baseball mind, a mind informed by pitcher probabilities, possibilities, and tendencies. He notes the positioning of the outfielders, he knows the game situation. If someone is on base, he knows the runner's strengths and weaknesses. His pitch recognition is outstanding, his decision-making superb. His awareness is total.

This is not idle conjecture, nor is it hype. It's not based solely on the opinions of scouts and other baseball gurus. Those human assessments are important, of course, but they have limitations and can be subjective. Mookie's baseball intellect was documented with clinical precision when he was a high school senior. He was an early subject in a cutting-edge system known as neuroscouting, a tool developed to rate a player's baseball mind, how fast and intuitive his baseball IQ is in real time. Among other things, neuroscouting reveals how well a player sees a pitch and how well he reads a pitch. Mookie was a star pupil, confirming, enhancing, and quantifying the observations of experienced scouts. So Betts not only ticks all the boxes with fans and scouts, he passes muster with science as well. More about that later.

Little wonder that whenever he enters the batter's box, Red

Sox fans' expectations rise along with the blood pressure of the opposing pitcher. The first pitch goes by and he looks at it and you can almost see the wheels turning. If the next pitch is an inside fastball, the right-handed Betts can whip the bat around with lightning speed and propel the ball down the left-field line. Outside pitches are treated with distain, unless they can be poked to right field. At Fenway, he ignores the beckoning siren of the Green Monster unless he can visit it on his own terms.

His hand-eye coordination is off the charts. He can react at the last split-second and still power the ball into the outfield and beyond. He's seldom fooled on a pitch, and if he is, it's a lesson learned, filed away for later use. Should you think that Betts's skills are robotic, you would be wrong. He has an intuition and an adaptability that artificial intelligence could never duplicate.

Descriptions of this man tend to the metaphorical. He's a ball-hawk in right field, a cheetah on the basepaths, and has cat-like reflexes at the plate. His arm is a cannon.

The *human* comparison that first comes to mind is Hank Aaron, especially considering his strong wrists and superior bat speed. But there's some Willie Mays in the baseball DNA as well, especially when he takes the field. On the basepaths Mookie is shrewd and swift. He doesn't steal bases in order to pad his stats. In fact, he may be one of the most unselfish players in a sport that heralds individual accomplishment. He takes a walk. He sacrifices, he does the little things that lead to the big inning. He's eminently coachable. His teammates love him. He is such a cheerleader in the dugout that he threatens to make Wally the Green Monster redundant.

Making the Team

With all this talent, it's easy to assume that the stars must have been perfectly aligned to make Betts a superstar. But that wasn't the case. Without the intervention of his mother, he might never have had a chance to prove himself.

For those who have experienced it, "choosing up" sides is one of those childhood rites of passage that tends to linger in the memory. For some it represents validation and acceptance, while for others it's the first hint that life isn't always fair.

Playground rules differ slightly according to geography, but the process went something like this: A group of guys (and/or gals) met at the ball field to play baseball on a Saturday morning. By some unwritten and unspoken law, the two best players were automatically the captains and accorded the honor of choosing teams, the object being to create more or less balanced sides. One captain tossed the bat, handle up, to the other, who grasped it in his fist. Each would in turn put his fist above the other and they would alternate fist grips until there was no further room. This is where regional variations creep in. In some case that would be it; the last fist got first choice of players. Other rules allowed for a captain to put three fingers between the fist and the bat knob. A third alternative was for the last one gripping the bat to throw it backwards over his shoulders. If it went at least five bat lengths, he would get first choice.

This highly ritualized tradition triggered a range of emotions from the exhilarating to the excruciating, depending on your level of talent. Names were shouted out and teams began to form behind each captain. Each name that wasn't yours cast judgement on your ability, your popularity. You studiously avoided eye contact with the captain, with your friends, with anyone, pretending that you could care less. Finally, if there were still spots available, your name would be called and the teams would be set. Sometimes there were no more spots. The experience either made you want to improve or take up another sport.

Mookie Betts, Gold Glove outfielder and reigning American League MVP, was that kid—the one who wasn't chosen, whose name wasn't called. The one left standing on the sidelines. In his case, the whole thing was somewhat more bureaucratic. There was no bat toss, no "three fingers" rule. The determination was made by Little League coaches—i.e. adults.

As a child, Markus Lynn Betts was so small that even his

extra-small pair of baseball pants were in constant danger of falling down. His mom solved the problem by fitting him out in suspenders. He chose the ones with Teenage Mutant Ninja Turtles on them. And his mom bought him a matching Ninja Turtle glove to complete the ensemble. Some might say that this early exposure to Michelangelo, Leonardo, Donatello, and Raphael inspired him to become the fielding artist he is today. Certainly, many of the catches that he has made in Fenway's right field canvas qualify as masterpieces.

But for Mookie's mom, thoughts of future glory were the last thing on her mind. She just wanted her son to play some baseball. Diana Collins was and is a force of nature. She was introduced to baseball while growing up in Paducah, Kentucky, where her grandfather carved out a baseball diamond on the family farm. "There wasn't much else to do," she admits. "So we played baseball and softball all the time." In high school, she became a star player on the softball team and also developed into a skilled bowler. Not surprisingly, her passion for sport and love of competition was passed on to her son. Family lore suggests that even as a toddler, Mookie had a disdain for walls, even the walls of his crib. "He'd always be saying, 'Ball? Ball? Ball?' that's what he always wanted to do," Collins *MassLive.com*'s told Jen McCaffrey in 2015. "He would run everywhere. He never walked," added Willie Betts, Mookie's father. "He figured it out, if you put him down, he'd start running. He would just run, run, run."[88]

From the time he was three years old, Markus played endless games of catch with his mother in the backyard and she saw steady improvement. He could catch and throw the ball better than much older kids. All that was lacking was some competition, some actual ballgames. When he was five years old, she took him to sign up for the Little League in their hometown of Murfreesboro. He was "small-framed and very underweight," Collins admitted years later, but she still wasn't prepared for such a quick rejection of her son.

As Diana told *The Tennessean*, the first coach that she approached was less than encouraging. "He said, 'No, I don't really think [so].

I really need some bigger kids. I've got enough small kids and I'm trying to balance my team out.'" She moved on to speak with other coaches, but each time they looked at Mookie the answer was the same. They wanted the big, athletic kids. Collins persisted. "I said, 'Give him a chance, because he really can play.'"[89] Her pleas fell on deaf ears, which was disappointing to her and crushing for her little boy. "Mookie was getting kind of discouraged," Collins told CNBC's *Make It*. "You know how kids are when they see some-body say 'No.'"[90]

At this point, most parents would have accepted this decision, albeit reluctantly, and returned home to wait another year. Not Diana. She could read the disappointment on her son's face. "Nobody wants to have me," she recalls him saying. It was an accurate observation but one she refused to accept. "Oh no, you're going to play," she promised little Markus.

Only then did an idea began to take shape. She assessed the situation and noticed that a number of other children were similarly being rejected because of their size. She marched up to the Little League coordinator and made a request that would set her son on the road to the major leagues. She asked if she could add another team to the league. She was told that she could, but only if she could find a coach. Thus began the short but significant coaching career of Diana Collins.

During the historic 2018 Red Sox season, Mookie reminisced about playing for his mom. "For me, it was very enjoyable because my mom was competitive the same way I was," he said. "She was into the games, trying to win. She instilled in me, 'Hey, we're trying to win the game even though we're young.'"

The potential was there for a feel-good movie. The script practically writes itself. "It's kind of a little sad story but we just gathered up everybody that nobody wanted and we just formed our own team," Collins says. "It didn't matter, I wanted my kid to play ball." It would be nice to report that this team of rejects went on to show the Murfreesboro Little League that heart means more than size, that skill and determination always triumph. Unfortunately, that part of any future *Mookie Betts Story* won't make it to the big screen. Despite Mookie's obvious skills, the team was mediocre at best and finished in last place with only a handful of wins. One of the wins, however, came against the first coach who had passed on Betts in favor of larger players. And Markus Betts contributed to that win by quickly retrieving a ball hit to the outfield and running it back to the infield to tag the runner. At least that one part of the story should definitely not be condemned to the cutting-room floor.

As a rookie coach, Diana's instruction wasn't limited to skill development. She knew that the key to success in any sport was learning how to compete and how to win. That included taking advantage of Mookie's speed in the infield. "I just remember there was one game where we couldn't get an out," Collins told Ian Browne of *MLB.com* in 2015. "All the kids had to bat. I said to Mookie, 'We need to get an out.' And his favorite words were, 'OK, mama.' The ball was hit to shortstop, and he caught it and ran to first and so he could be the guy, and he slid into first and tagged the base. It was funny."[91]

Mookie still remembers the slightly unorthodox strategy years later. "We were four or five at the time, so they would hit a ground ball and instead of me throwing it to first, I was fast enough to just run over and tag 'em."

Early on, Diana and her husband Willie Betts taught their son about the concept of team play. In Little League there's often a huge disparity in talent level on any given team. Diana drummed it into her charges that you "don't criticize or critique your teammates if they're having a hard time. You try to encourage them just like you hope that they'll encourage you." Mookie took the advice to heart, serving as a "mini-coach" and making it his mission to maintain team morale. He continues that mission with the Red Sox. Every time a teammate homers, he greets him at the top step of the dugout and ceremoniously removes the batter's helmet.

Diana didn't fit the cliché of the pushy parent who lives out her own baseball dreams through her son. Both parents could be tough, but they were always fair. "[Mom] was going to let me play any sport I wanted to play, but if I was going to play she wanted to make sure I would learn all the basics. We weren't going to be bad at anything. If we were going to do it, we were going to be good at it."[92]

Her only stipulation was that once Mookie committed to something, he should see it through. Betts recalls, "One thing that stands out is when I was younger I wanted to quit football and I talked to her and she didn't let me. I thank her for not letting me. It taught me a life lesson that once you start something, you've got to finish it. She's taught me a lot of life lessons outside of sports."

Collins's first year of Little League coaching proved to be her last (although she later went on to coach women's slow-pitch teams for many years). The following year she turned over the coaching reins to someone else. Ironically, Mookie was partly responsible for her short tenure at the helm and she almost became a victim of her own coaching success. He hit a frozen rope line drive straight at her in a practice session, causing her to hit the deck. "It was a rocket," she told Ian Browne. "I said, 'It's time for me to get out of here.' My reflexes are not what they used to be."[93] But the path was set. She had persisted against bureaucratic indifference and Mookie was on his way to baseball stardom. All because she believed in him as only a mother can.

From that point forward, Diana and Willie, a Vietnam War veteran who worked as a mechanical superintendent for CSX Transportation for 30 years, supported their son at every level and in every sport. Although Diana and Willie separated when Mookie was eight years old, Willie routinely drove him to games and practices and stayed to watch him play.

Even today, when the Boston Red Sox boast one of the finest, most innovative coaching staffs in all of baseball, Mookie receives periodic advice, counsel, and even some constructive criticism from his first coach. On those occasions he sometimes tries to gently tell her that the major-league game differs considerably from the Little League version. That doesn't stop Diana Collins from phoning after a game to discuss his performance. "I don't care if it's different or not—explain it to me," Collins will insist. "He tells me all the time, 'OK, Ma, I'll call you later.'" But that line doesn't work with mothers, especially mothers like Diana. "No, I wanna talk now—you just don't want to hear it," she tells him. "I commend Mookie and pat him on the back when he does well, but you also need to hear, 'You need to work on this.' You've got to hear the good and the bad. You can't just praise kids all the time and then [they] never hear the other side of it." And Mookie Betts, ever the good son, listens patiently as his mother and former coach critiques his game.

From the beginning, the two have had the kind of loving relationship that allows for growth and interdependence within a supportive environment. "She wanted whatever I wanted," Mookie told *Sporting News* contributor Gary Phillips. "From me being a little kid, she always said that I would say that I wanted to be a professional baseball player. She did whatever it took to make that come true."[94]

A Close Call

Even with Diana in his corner, Mookie might never have fulfilled his childhood dream without the timely help of a guardian angel. In the spring of 2005, along with three teammates, the 12-year-old was on a road trip to a bowling tournament. His stepfather was driving the family's SUV while his mother occupied the passenger seat and the boys snoozed in the back. Suddenly, the car struck a utility pole and careened across the busy interstate, finally coming to rest upside down next to the median.

Diana could see the other kids scramble through a window but Mookie, who had been seated behind the driver and not wearing a seat belt, had been thrown from the vehicle. Ignoring her badly broken shoulder, Diana tried frantically to open the door. Once outside, she looked around at the chaotic scene but couldn't locate Mookie until finally she heard him screaming for his mother. She followed the voice and a few desperate moments later spotted him lying face down and stunned in the path of rush-hour traffic. For Diana, the sequence of events seemed to play out in slow motion. She knew that if the traffic wasn't stopped, a car would roll over her son.

Like an answered prayer, a man seemed to appear out of nowhere, got out of his car, and carried Mookie to safety, away from the oncoming traffic. The man then halted the two-way traffic until emergency vehicles and paramedics arrived. The emergency workers quickly cut away Mookie's clothing and checked him over for internal injuries. Years later he had only sporadic memories of the accident. "I don't remember anything except them cutting my clothes off," he told Jessica Camerato of *Boston.com* in 2014. "Those were some good clothes. That was a good pair of jeans and a bowling shirt."[95] For once, Diana hadn't been able to protect her boy. "To this day I don't know who saved him," she told *Sports Illustrated*'s Tom Verducci in 2015. "He was God's little angel."[96] As for Mookie, the sixth grader escaped with a broken jaw and an assortment of scrapes and bruises from head to foot, including a dislocated wrist and broken toes. Only his braces saved his teeth from snapping off. There were no fatalities, but Betts's stepfather had to be airlifted to the hospital.

The traumatic incident left more than physical scars. After a week in hospital in Kansas City, Mookie was deemed well enough to go home, although his broken jaw required a liquid diet. When his stepfather went to get him, Mookie discovered that he had developed a fear of riding in cars. "Me and my mom were terrified of riding in the car at that point," he told Camerato. Every bump in the road brought him back to the scene of the accident. "We tried to go to sleep and couldn't." Even a decade and a half later, certain situations will trigger his anxiety. "If you hit the little ridges on the side of the street, I'll flip out and I won't go back to sleep."[97]

Predictably, Mookie didn't embrace the role of invalid. He wanted to get back to sports: baseball, bowling, basketball, track, it didn't matter. Even the cumbersome cast he was forced to wear couldn't stop him. He practiced playing basketball with his left hand. As for baseball, he had a strategy for that too. "My wrist took the longest. I couldn't throw because it [the cast] was on my right hand, but I could hit . . . Then you had a DH [designated hitter] and an EH [extra hitter]—I was the EH. I put a batting glove on, had my bat, and I could kind of wrap my hand around it and I hit. I literally played in games with a cast on my wrist. I don't know how I did it."

The near-death experience wasn't going to stop Mookie. He worked extra hard and was soon batting, fielding, and throwing as if nothing had happened. If anything, the accident made him stronger, gave him a new perspective on life. "You can't take anything for granted," he says. "Life can be taken from you at any time. Try to be happy. Anything can happen at any time."

Even today, it's clearly painful for Diana Collins to talk about the accident. "The worst part was him being ejected from the vehicle. That was pretty bad. It's a memory that you don't want to have but yeah, it happened and it was horrific. He was little and he does remember the accident, but there were things he doesn't remember and that's probably good. When you're young, you can rebound from a lot of things. So maybe it was a blessing that he was so young."

Mookie's Mom: An Interview with Diana Collins

It was January of 2019 and Diana Collins already had things in perspective. Just two months earlier Diana's son, Mookie Betts, had led the Boston Red Sox to the World Series, which they won in five games against the LA Dodgers. He had been named to the American League All-Star team and was among the league leaders in virtually every offensive and defensive category. After the season, the awards and accolades began to pour in. He captured his third Gold Glove for his spectacular play in right field. He won his second Silver Slugger award. And then he topped it off with his selection as American League MVP. The authors spoke with Diana about what it's like to be Mookie Betts's mother. It's not hard to see where Mookie got his personality and his love of sport. Both parents were supportive of his athletic pursuits, although the passion for baseball stems mostly from the Collins side of the family.

Diana acknowledges her son's skills and accomplishments, but you quickly get the impression that it's the way he plays the game and lives his life that makes her most proud.

(Note: The day after our interview, Mookie Betts signed a one-year, $20 million contract with the Red Sox.)

Q: Which of Mookie's on-field and off-field accomplishments are you proudest of?

A: I take pride in all aspects of Mookie's life. I'd just like to see him keep going and doing what he's doing. One of the things that you have to realize is that when it's a team sport, team is not "I," it's "we." Being part of a team means that you have to work together, and that's something Mookie learned early on. If we're going to play as a team, then we will win as a team or we'll lose as a team. You always want your teammates to do well. That's something I always emphasized when I coached his Little League team. I tried to impress it on all the kids. To me that's one of the first things that coaches should teach kids—the concept of team. And the concept of sportsmanship and getting along with others. To be a good team player, you have to learn to get along with people and be a good listener. All those things come into play whatever the level of competition.

So I'm proud of everything Mookie does, on the field and off. It's the complete person that he's become in all aspects of his life. I wouldn't single out any one thing that ranks over others. It depends on the time and situation. He loves people, he's got a big heart. Sometimes you're proud of this, sometimes of that. I just take pride in seeing him continue to move in the right direction, and now he'll be instilling those qualities in his little girl as well.

Q: Mookie is part of an incredible Red Sox outfield. They work so well together and it looks like they have so much fun out there. What's the key to that relationship?

A: The Red Sox outfielders absolutely have a special bond. They work so well together and complement one another. There's a mutual respect between the three of them, no question. It's a wonderful thing when you know that your teammates have your back. It's really all about chemistry and that's what they have. Mookie, Andrew, and Jackie hang around together off the field as well, after games and during their off time. It's a tight bond. They do a lot of things together when they're on road trips—going to movies, or whatever. You'll find them eating together a lot. When you see them work together and play together, it's obvious they enjoy each other's company and the bond becomes even stronger.

Q: How well do you know Benintendi and Bradley Jr.?

A: I know Andrew and Jackie well. Their moms and dads and I have all connected as parents. In fact, you'll often see us all go out for family dinners together before a game or between games. Our families really click. So the chemistry is definitely there and that's such an important thing.

Benintendi is a relatively quiet guy but he has some humor in him, too. He knows what he's doing out there. He's poised and he wants to win. He's just a really nice guy, a genuine guy who always gives 100 percent and let's face it, those kinds of players are hard to find. His spirit is there for everyone to see.

Jackie and Mookie played together before they came up to the majors, so I've known Jackie for quite a long period, longer than any other Red Sox player. That makes a difference. I see him all the time and we talk all the time. And of course, he always greets me with, "Hi Mom, whatcha doin'?" or "Hey Mom, how's it goin'?" Jackie is a very special kid.

Q: They always seem to support each other. It was obvious last year when Jackie was in the midst of his hitting slump.

A: Again, I think the team is always pulling for one another, so they were trying to figure it out together because with Jackie the talent is obviously there, the skill is definitely there—and so [the question is] what can we do to come out of this slump. It's never a case of anyone ever thinking they're going to give up on anyone, at any time. Jackie has the drive and he has the ability, so . . . it was just one of those droughts that we all wanted him to come out of.

Q: Who else is Mookie especially close to on the current team?

A: Mookie is very close to J. D. [Martinez] and he talks a lot with Xander [Bogaerts]. J. D. just joined the team last year, but he and Mookie just hit it off from the beginning. Same with Xander as well. J. D. is not a selfish player. He hits well and he wants you to hit well—if you're on his team. He's always willing to share a hitting tip. This is the kind of team that's not afraid to step out and encourage one another and figure things out together. They easily give out tips on how to make your game better. It's important. Some people wouldn't do that; not all players would volunteer to help. Some just keep it to themselves. But I don't see this Red Sox team ever being like that.

Q: It's refreshing that there are no oversized egos in the group.

A: It's not a matter of ego. It's all about self-confidence, believing in yourself and your talent, and what you have the potential to do. And then you step forward. It's not about being a braggart or having a big ego—just a healthy self-confidence about what you can do with your skill set.

Q: Most players have long-term goals. As a young player, Ted Williams said he wanted to become the greatest hitter who ever lived. Does Mookie think in those terms?

A: I think Mookie is living in the moment right now and he'll worry about retirement when that time comes. Maybe then he'll look down the road at what he's accomplished when he nears that point. Because right now you're just trying to do what you can do to reach your full value and let your spark be what it is. He wants to be in the now.

To be in the same realm or in the same conversation with some of the greats of the past is outstanding; I think he treasures that to the utmost. If it happens down the road that he lives up to that standard, then I think that's outstanding. But I wouldn't say that that's what his goal is. His goal is to be the best Mookie he can be.

Q: Which of Mookie's many incredible defensive gems has impressed you most?

A: He's had a couple of catches that stand out, but one of my favorites was when the pitcher was going for a no-hitter and he pulled the ball back in from over the fence. That was one of my all-time favorites. [Author's note: On September 25, 2015, Rich Hill was pitching a two-hitter. Baltimore's Chris Davis hit a ball to the fence that Betts nabbed for the final out to preserve the 7–0 shutout.] He's made several running catches that I loved because I played sports and people think it's easy when you run and catch the ball but you have to judge the ball and time the ball. There's a lot that goes into catching that ball. It's not as easy as people think so . . . So he's had several favorites, but to actually go over the fence and come back with the ball—that to me says a lot. You have to believe you can do it and then do it.

Q: It's pretty well-known that you got Mookie started in baseball. Where did your love of the game come from?

A: Growing up, my grandfather was a sharecropper and we had acres and acres of land and when you grow up in the country, pretty much all you have to do is play sports. We didn't have lots of money so we didn't have a lot of other things we could do and sports was something we could do and that's what we did. I grew up playing sports.

My grandfather made us our own ball diamond on the farm. There were enough of us grandkids to play games and we always had a couple of other close friends join in, so altogether we had enough to make two full teams. We could play against each other all the time and that's how you learned to play the game. You never wanted to be the worst one out there, so you always tried to improve.

I was going to go to college on a softball scholarship but my momma didn't want me to go that far from home so I quit after high school. But I played around here [Paducah] and I coached ladies' slow-pitch for about 10 years.

Q: What about Mookie's father [Willie Betts]?

A: Mookie's dad ran track and played basketball and so he helped him with that. He also played some pickup ball but nothing close to my family.

Q: Does your son know how far Red Sox Nation extends and how closely fans follow his every move?

A: Mookie realizes that there are many true Boston fans and that they're all over the country, all over the world. He hears about that and sees it when the team travels. Boston has been good to Mookie and to the Red Sox. He takes all the fuss in stride. Mookie just wants to play ball. He can adapt to any city.

Mookie was 10 years old when he and his mother moved from Murfreesboro to the Nashville suburb of Brentwood. Although he and Diana divorced, Willie Betts lived nearby and continued to be active in his son's life, driving him to two or three sports events a month. Later, during baseball games at Nashville's John Overton High School, the elder Betts manned the ticket gates while Diana Collins worked at the concession stand.[98] The retired railroad man punctuated every great play with a blast from a toy train whistle.

During those playing days at Overton, Mookie was a middle infielder alternating between second baseman and shortstop. He hit .548 in his junior year and stole 24 bases. In his senior year, he fell a bit short of that—.508, but upped his stolen base total to 30.

It was at Overton that his coach, Mike Morrison, took note of his amazing ability to absorb and analyze baseball instruction and immediately incorporate it into his game. Collins credits her former husband with passing that ability along to Mookie. "They both can pick up stuff. He can probably fix anything. They [can] just watch stuff and be able to fix a hole or repair something. It goes beyond sports."

Hedging Your Betts: Scouting Mookie

Like choosing a spouse, scouting young ballplayers is an inexact science. On the surface the prospect may look great, but not until you see them under pressure, on a bad day, over an extended period of time, do you know if you've made a good decision. By then it's often too late. Danny Watkins was an area scout covering Tennessee, Alabama, and Mississippi for the Boston Red Sox. He first saw Mookie Betts in the early summer of 2010, watching him perform at a high school baseball showcase at Middle Tennessee State University. Betts didn't stand out physically, but Watkins thought he saw something that many other observers missed. He saw his finesse around second base, easily handling a hard grounder and flipping it behind his back to the bag to force the runner. He also noted his explosive swing and ability to get the barrel of the bat on the ball.

Back when average-sized players were the norm, the Aarons and Mayses and Musials and Kalines and Yastrzemskis stood out as first among equals. We're now in an era when size really does matter in the selection of ballplayers. Average-sized players are often overlooked in favor of the Aaron Judges, Giancarlo Stantons, and Mike Trouts. There are exceptions, of course, and talent often wins out, but put a player like Dustin Pedroia, José Altuve, or Jimmy Rollins in a group with the athletic giants and see who emerges with the higher draft position. The rule of thumb seems to be that the higher the player height-wise, the higher he is drafted.

It's fair to say that Danny Watkins deserves the thanks of every Red Sox fan. Like the old prospector who lets it slip that he's discovered a rather large gold nugget—or perhaps fool's gold—Watkins had the attention of the Red Sox. A veritable rush of scouts made their way to Overton High School during Mookie's senior year, each one generating more paperwork, more opinions. Cross-checker Mike Rikard (now Red Sox VP of Amateur Scouting) saw Mookie at another showcase just two months later. He was impressed and said so in his report, but reminded himself that this was a high school player batting against high school pitching.

Scouts spend their entire careers out on a limb and before sending in their scouting report, they want to be as sure as possible that they have a safety net beneath them. To that end, the scouting profession developed a phrase that mitigates their responsibility. On the one hand, the strategic phrase keeps expectations under control, and on the other it suggests that the scout might be conservative in his assessments. Some would call it covering your a**. Scouts say, "I might be light."

Every Red Sox scout who saw the young Mookie echoed the line until it became a mantra, a chorus of cautions. They obviously loved what they saw, but it was as if they didn't trust their own eyes. Was he really that good? Watkins watched him make those smooth defensive infield plays that fateful June day and his jaw dropped. "I looked around to see, 'Did anybody see that?'" Watkins told Brian MacPherson of the *Providence Journal*. No one did. Or at least no other scout dared to pass the word up the line to their major-league club.

It was then scouting director Amiel Sawdaye's job (he is now Senior VP and Assistant Manager with the Arizona Diamondbacks) to not only read the scouting reports but to read between the lines of the scouting reports. "Almost every guy wrote, 'I might be light here,'" he told MacPherson. Sawdaye saw though their cautions and felt their enthusiasm jumping from the pages. "Maybe you don't see this guy against good pitching. Maybe you don't have a ton of history. But you're like, 'Man, this guy does everything we like. Maybe I'm underestimating how good he is.'"[99]

Neuroscouting

The Red Sox organization also hedged its bets by breaking out a revolutionary new approach to evaluating players called neuroscouting. Then Red Sox general manager Theo Epstein, the man who engineered the end of the 86-year-old world championship drought known to some as the Curse of the Bambino, decided to add some completely impartial input to the scouting reports. Mookie was destined to be one of the pioneers.

Danny Watkins was a frequent visitor to Overton High School during Mookie's senior year. He came to watch his discovery play basketball and run track in addition to monitoring his progress on the diamond. One day he showed up unannounced and took Mookie from class to explain the basics of neuroscouting to him. He asked if he would become part of the pilot project and Betts agreed to sacrifice his lunch period to the furtherance of science.

Watkins invited the young ballplayer to play a series of computer games, not a tough ask for a young teenager. These games were not your usual strategic quests, however. They were a battery of painstakingly developed, science-based, state-of-the-art baseball challenges designed to measure the previously unmeasurable.

Amateur scouting has been around since professional baseball began, but it's always been subjective, with teams depending on the judgment and analytical skills of their scouts, often retired ballplayers. The most outstanding scouts have the ability to look at the flaws of raw youth and see beyond them to the player's potential. Countless Hall of Famers have been discovered in this traditional way. Many will argue that attitude and desire and other so-called "intangibles" are best observed and assessed through personal relationships. Overall, the system worked well and there will always be a place for it in the game. On the skills side, it's relatively easy for an experienced scout to assess a player's swing. Such things as bat speed, technique, and mechanics are all tangible, or at least identifiable elements in a hitter's skill set. But what about pitch recognition and decision-making?

Mookie was among the first to undergo the testing process, and no doubt the developers of the early neuroscouting models were forced to recalibrate the process after his performance that day at Overton. The highly sophisticated battery of computer exercises covered things that even the most seasoned, eagle-eyed scout couldn't hope to capture through naked eye observation. Mookie was instructed to follow the commands and not worry about the results. "I did what I could," he told Alex Speier of the *Boston Globe* in 2015. One element was designed to register a player's ability to pick up the spin on the ball. Horizontal spins had to be differenti-ated from vertical spins, all in a split second. "It was just like, a ball popped up, tap space bar as fast as you could. If the seams were one way, you tapped it. If it was the other way, you weren't supposed to tap it. I was getting some of them wrong. I wasn't getting frustrated but I was like, 'Dang, this is hard.'"[100]

The pitch recognition aspect was multifaceted. One activity required the test subject to tap the space bar as soon as he deter-mined that the pitch would be in the strike zone. Another featured a curveball that blinked red if it was going to be out of the zone. The challenge was to recognize this as a ball instantaneously.

The topper was an activity that allowed for every possible pitch: fastball, curve, changeup, and sinker. Not only was Mookie supposed to hit the ball but he was asked to hit it *to all fields*.

Very wisely, neuroscouting also attempts to assess the charac-ter of the player being tested. To that end, certain errors are built into the program. If a player is frustrated or makes excuses based on the irregularities, the theory is that he's likely to be a complainer in the majors; if he ignores such errors and continues to perform, he's more likely to handle the ups and downs of major-league sea-sons. Not surprisingly, Betts scored incredibly high in all aspects of the test—"ridiculously high," according to one source.

This was one of many factors that led Theo Epstein to draft Betts in 2011. It was Epstein's last season as Red Sox GM before moving over to the Chicago Cubs.

Mookie Betts was the perfect example of a player who had all the tools, ticked all the boxes, and met all the criteria but was still in danger of being passed over. Why? Even though his talent had been carefully measured by every available yardstick, he lacked the "wow" factor. Part of that was his size and power. He was 5-foot-9 and 165 pounds at the time, and understandably didn't have all eyes turn to him when he came to the plate. He had the tools, but he didn't have what Watkins has called "the sexy tools." "He was one of those guys who could easily kind of blend in," he told Christopher Smith of *Masslive.com*.[101] Should the Red Sox make an all-out effort to sign him or allow him to marinate in the university ranks for a few years?

The Red Sox were in the market for impact players. Did Mookie qualify as an impact player? Not yet, maybe, but Watkins had a "gut feel" for Mookie and sometimes you just have to go with that. He liked this kid a lot. Liked everything about him, the way he played the game and the way he respected the game. Watkins felt that the potential reward outweighed the risk.

Amiel Sawdaye was armed with all this Mookie data and meta Mookie data, both human- and computer-generated, when he attended the 2011 June draft. All that aside, one of the biggest factors at play when selecting a player is signability. Teams don't want to pick a player and then discover that he won't sign a contract. If a player chosen in the first 10 rounds opts not to sign, his slot value is still counted against that team's bonus pool. In 2011, penalties were put in place for teams that went over the signing bonus pool. On the other hand, they knew there was also interest from the Kansas City Royals and San Diego Padres and perhaps as many as four other teams. Even then, Sawdaye held off until the fifth round before deciding to put his faith in the enthusiasm of his scouts and the evidence of science, making Mookie their 172nd pick overall.

Mookie had been watching the draft from back home in Tennessee and when he was passed over in the second round figured he wasn't going to be selected at all. From that point he watched with waning interest until the phone rang before the fifth round had begun. It was the Red Sox calling to try to assess the chances of Betts actually signing if he were drafted. Watkins explained the process to Christopher Smith. "The way the draft has evolved with the slotted values, it becomes such a priority to sign those first 10-round guys," he said. "We don't negotiate or come to terms with anyone before we draft them. But there's got to be a comfort level." That comfort level was reached during the phone call.

Mookie had committed to a baseball scholarship with the University of Tennessee, but when the Red Sox drafted him and offered him a $750,000 signing bonus, he consulted with his family and made the decision to turn pro. The bonus was about $600,000 above the slot value.

Mookie in the Minors

The Red Sox sent Mookie to Fort Myers for instructional league work in the fall of 2011 and that's where he first met his future outfield neighbor, Jackie Bradley Jr. Jackie was already a bona fide star, having just led South Carolina to a second consecutive College World Series championship in which he was named Most Outstanding Player. Betts admits to being star-struck when he first encountered the major leaguer-in-waiting. They were assigned as roommates. "I was in awe," he said in 2018. "I watched the College World Series and then I walked into my hotel room at instructs and Jackie's there. It took me a second to kind of realize I didn't want to be a fan boy at the time."[102]

The fact that they have some shared history as both roommates and teammates made their eventual reunion with the Red Sox seamless and no doubt hastened Mookie's transition to the outfield. "We may not have come up together, but we came through the same ranks and through the same teams. We get to talk about our stories. It's one of those things where I can stand next to him and know that we've kind of been together every step of the way. I knew what kind of player he is. He's proven it. He definitely proved it in this series. He's not just a glove out there. He can do it all."[103] No doubt some of those stories revolve around their sharing a room. For some reason all the players congregated in their room to play video games, perhaps because it was the cleanest. The downside was that the two never had a chance to nap or relax. Even after they ceased to play, the rest of the team hung out there, often until 1:00 or 2:00 in the morning.

Mookie also appeared in a single game for the Gulf Coast League Red Sox in 2011 but made the best of the opportunity, playing shortstop and going 2-for-4 while racking up two runs batted in and a stolen base. But on defense, he bombed, committing three errors in six chances, a subject that might also arise when he and Jackie Jr., two Gold Glove winners, reminisce about 2011.

In 2012, Betts played the full season in the New York-Penn League. In 71 games for the Lowell Spinners (58 at second base and 13 at shortstop), he hit .267 (with a .352 on-base percentage), failed to hit a home run, and drove in 31 runs. He did cut down on the errors, though, compiling a .958 fielding percentage.

While the Boston Red Sox were winning the World Series in 2013 (with JBJ, Mookie's roomie from the Instructional League picking up a ring), Betts was finishing off a split season during which he played second base exclusively for two teams in Single-A ball. He began the year in South Carolina with the Greenville Drive (South Atlantic League) and played there from April 5 to July 7, hitting .296 and, more importantly, achieving a .418 on-base percentage, with eight homers and 26 RBIs. Usually batting leadoff, he scored 63 runs in 76 games. At one point, he had a 19-game hitting streak. He was selected to play in the league's All-Star Game.

From July 9 through the end of the season on September 2, he played in "High-A" ball for the Salem (Virginia) Red Sox in the Carolina League. In 51 games with Salem, he hit .341 (.414 OBP) with seven homers and 39 RBIs and swiped 38 bases on the year. In one game in Myrtle Beach, he went 5-for-6 with two homers and seven RBIs—"a pretty good day," says Mookie. Betts was named both the Breakout Player of the Year in the Red Sox minor-league system and the Offensive Player of the Year. He credited his dramatic improvement in batting to Greenville hitting coach U. L.

Washington, who had him lower his leg kick when he stepped into his swing.[104]

That fall, he appeared in 16 Arizona Fall League games and hit .271 for the Surprise Saguaros. He was named to play in the league's Fall Stars Game. Tim Hyers tells a story about Mookie in the Fall League in 2013. He was in the dugout in Arizona with the Red Sox minor-league hitting coordinator. "We're talking about outfielders. Mookie would shag every so often in the outfield. We were just talking about players and who could do in the outfield—this was before they made the transition. The coaching staff were all in there talking. 'You got some good defenders, some good outfielders,' and one of the coaches piped up with, 'Hey, our best outfielder's Mookie Betts.' Everybody just laughed. 'You see him out there shagging every day? He's the best outfielder we have on the team.' That just tells you the caliber of athlete that he was."

He'd earned a promotion to the next rung on the ladder—Double A—and started 2014 playing for the Eastern League's Portland Sea Dogs, geographically and psychologically nearer to Boston's Fenway Park. He played 40 games at second base, but already the Red Sox were beginning to transition him to outfield work. He played an even dozen games in center field. Appearing in 54 games in all, he improved his offensive game, hitting .355 (.443 OBP) with an OPS of .994. He now had the full attention of the Red Sox decision-makers.

On May 10, he went 0-for-4, notable in that it was the first time all year that he had not reached base. It ended a streak that had extended back into 2013 with Salem—he had reached base safely, one way or another, in 66 consecutive regular-season games. Counting the five postseason games in which he played, Betts had reached base in 71 consecutive games. Though he failed to reach base in the May 10 game, he did drive in two runs, both on groundouts.[105] He was leading the Eastern League in batting when he was promoted to Triple-A Pawtucket (International League).

It was on a road trip to Scranton that Mookie experienced the charms of minor-league cities. The team was staying at a hotel that had the reputation of being haunted. The team had read all about it and late that night decided to go looking for ghosts. "I probably got only four or five hours of sleep all night," says Betts. Little did he know that while he was searching for spirits, his teammates were conjuring up some mischief. "I came back to my room and I heard some shuffling." Being more of a fencebuster than a ghostbuster, he did the sensible thing. "I started packing my stuff because I was going to leave. By the time I got to the door I was scared out of my mind. They got me good."

The incident didn't seem to hurt him at the plate. With the PawSox, he hit in 23 consecutive games starting on June 3 and before the month was out, he got the call that every ballplayer dreams of. He was going to the majors.

Different Balls, Different Strikes

Interestingly, the sport-rich DNA that Diana passed along to her son had a strand that included a bowling component. For Mookie, bowling is much more than a weekend diversion from the stresses of Major League Baseball. Competing in a tournament with his mother, he won his first bowling trophy when he was just eight years old. In 2010 he was named Tennessee Boys Bowler of the Year and recorded a 290-point game. Even the historic 2018 baseball World Series wasn't Mookie's first. In November 2017 at the Professional Bowling Association World Series of Bowling in Reno, Nevada, he bowled a perfect 300-point game, one of four on his résumé. He is so good that he has expressed interest in someday joining the PBA tour.

Mookie excelled in many sports. As a high school hoopster player at Overton, the 5-foot-9 guard was MVP of the District 12-AAA League and Class-AAA All-City Player of the Year in the Nashville metropolitan area.[106] Overton High School coach Mike Morrison said Mookie could excel in almost anything: "You'd go play ping pong with him and he'd whip your tail in ping pong because his eye-hand coordination was superior to most kids and any of us around here really."[107]

MLB Welcomes MLB

The 2013 Red Sox had won the World Series, probably the most unexpected of the four twenty-first century world championships they have added to the five they managed to win in the early part of the twentieth century (1903, 1912, 1915, 1916, 1918).

The 2014 team lacked the spark shown the previous season and in late June they were mired in fourth place in the American League East, seven games behind the first-place Toronto Blue Jays and five back of the Yankees. The yo-yo-ing Sox had finished dead last in 2012 before their surprising revival the following year. They were destined to visit the AL East basement again in 2014 (they also finished last in 2015, before rebounding to first place in 2016, 2017, and 2018). At the precise halfway mark in the season, their record stood at 37–44 and it was obvious to everyone that they needed an infusion of fresh new talent.

They were in the midst of a series at Yankee Stadium when they decided to unveil their hottest young prospect in the media capital of the world. Mookie Betts was only 21 years old, but the stories of his potential preceded him to the majors. He was still known as a second baseman, but insiders knew his future was in Fenway's outfield. Coach Arnie Beyeler worked with both Brock Holt and Mookie Betts during the 2014 season, helping them both develop more outfield skills, so they could transition from being infielders to outfielders.

Mookie was still primarily a second baseman, but the outfield experimentation that had begun in Portland had continued after his promotion to Triple-A Pawtucket. The Red Sox had a solid second baseman in Dustin Pedroia and felt that the quickest path to the majors for Mookie was in the outfield. With Pawtucket, he would play more outfield than second base. He started with the PawSox on June 3. He reached base safely in each of his first 22 games with the Rhode Island affiliate, batting .322 though June 27. Coming on the heels of his 66-game on-base streak that had just been snapped in Portland, it's fair to say that Betts had the full attention of the Red Sox brass.

Mookie was glad to transition to becoming an outfielder, said Red Sox hitting coach Tim Hyers. Tim had been a scout for the Red Sox from 2009 to 2012 and minor-league hitting coordinator from 2013 to 2015. From 2016 to 2017, he served as assistant hitting coach for the Los Angeles Dodgers, then came back to Boston for the 2018 season. He'd seen all these guys early on.

"I saw all of them come up. I was there the first day that Benintendi was drafted and I came in really the first full year for Mookie. Jackie had been in the organization, I think, about a year, a little over a year before I got there. I was the [minor-league] hitting coordinator. I was there for Mookie's first day in New York. He'd come up as a second baseman. He was in Yankee Stadium. He'd had four starts in right field in the minor leagues.

"I think he wanted to play in the big leagues. He's the type of player who wants to do anything to help the team. I think it was a twofold. He wanted to help the team and get to the big leagues as fast as possible. That was a route. And he wanted to help the team, do whatever they asked him to do."

In the not-too-distant past, rushing a player to the majors was deemed foolhardy in the extreme, even dangerous to the player's development. The argument was that a player's confidence could be ruined beyond repair if he failed on the big-league stage. The *Globe*'s Christopher Gasper had already warned against rushing the "uber-prospect" to the majors. Not having been a first-round pick, he never really got the attention that some of those players did. Early in the 2014 season, reporters started noticing. During an interview as he began the season in the minors, he said, "Going from last year, really not getting interviewed at all, to now having some interviews once a week or so, it's different . . . It was fun, exciting kind of going from not being anybody, not necessarily that I'm somebody now, but just kind of a name that's buzzing a little bigger."[108]

As long as he was getting on base, there was always a chance to do more. "I just try to get on base no matter what. Whether it be walk, hit, error, whatever. Because I feel like I affect the game with my legs—stealing bags, scoring runs."

He continued to get on base a lot. The 66-game on-base streak, begun the year before, lasted until mid-May 2014. He was soon promoted to Pawtucket and reached base in every one of his first 16 games.

On June 24, Betts was named to the All-Star Futures Game to be played on July 13 at Target Field. Red Sox outfielder Shane Victorino's minor-league rehab work was suspended indefinitely on June 27; it was clear that the Flyin' Hawaiian wasn't coming back to the Red Sox outfield any time soon. Meanwhile, Mookie Betts was learning the position and was also burning up the basepaths, with 28 steals on the season to that point.

In total, he stole 54 bases during his time in Portland, Pawtucket, and Boston in 2014.

Betts was called up on June 28 and joined the team in New York where the Red Sox were playing the Yankees. GM Ben Cherington said, "I don't think we can be gun-shy about calling up a guy we believe in. We also wouldn't call someone up who we didn't feel could be successful right away."[109]

Starting his career in New York against the Yankees meant immediate and total immersion into the rivalry often called the most intense in pro sports. Since that dark day when Babe Ruth was sold by the Red Sox to the Yankees after the 1919 season, the histories of the two original AL franchises have been intertwined. DiMaggio and Williams, Fisk and Munson, Boggs and Mattingly, Jeter and Garciaparra: there were always opposing players who personified the competition between the two teams.

Betts was destined to be the new face of the Red Sox (just as Aaron Judge has since become the new face of the Yankees), and it was only appropriate that the archrival Yankees were the opposition when Betts got his first major-league hit. With Yankee Stadium as the stage, the scene couldn't have been scripted any better. Mookie's mother, father, and fiancée were sitting together at the game. He was playing right field, with Jackie Bradley Jr. in center and Daniel Nava in left. It was the first time that MLB and

JBJ, former Instructional League roomies, had played in the out-field together.

Mookie batted eighth in the lineup that day, in front of JBJ. The Red Sox scored first, in the top of the second, when Stephen Drew hit a one-out single to right field, scoring Mike Napoli. Betts came up to bat for the first time in the big leagues and grounded into a 5-4-3 double play.

A three-run third-inning homer by David Ortiz staked the Sox to a 4–0 lead, but the Yankees scored in the bottom of the inning to get them on the board. Solo homers by Mark Teixeira and Carlos Beltran made it 4–3.

Digging in against Yankees starting pitcher Chase Whitley in the top of the fourth, the Red Sox rookie rapped a hard-hit single up the middle. In the crowd a TV camera captured Diana Collins, surrounded by Yankees fans, pumping her fist in an expression of unbridled joy. To put a cherry on top of a perfect day, Yankees shortstop and future Hall of Famer Derek Jeter, realizing the sig-nificance of the hit, retrieved the ball and rolled it to the dugout for the budding superstar. Mookie was thrown out trying to steal sec-ond but was philosophical about it in the postgame scrum. "They told me, don't change anything, so I'll take that here and try to be aggressive and steal bases," he said.[110]

Bradley drew a walk to lead off the fifth and the next two bat-ters also reached on bases on balls. Dustin Pedroia singled to right, scoring Jackie, for his third RBI of the game. In the bottom of the inning, Ichiro Suzuki hit a triple to right field and later scored. The triple was the result of what one writer called an "ill-advised" attempt by Betts to make a shoestring catch in right. It was only the third time that Mookie had played right field in the minors or majors. With the score 7–5 Red Sox, Betts walked to lead off the sixth and Bradley singled to left. After Brock Holt singled to load the bases and Nava struck out, Betts scored on a sac fly by Pedroia to make it 8–5, the final score.

Four days later, on July 2, Mookie notched his first hit at

Fenway Park and once again Betts's mom and dad and girlfriend Brianna were there to see it. The hit, which also happened to be his first career home run, was a two-run shot into the Monster seats against Carlos Villanueva in the fifth inning of an interleague game with the Chicago Cubs. In cases like this, every attempt is made to find the fan who caught the ball and retrieve the treasured piece of memorabilia for the young player. That wasn't a problem because the fan who caught Mookie's first career dinger happened to be Chris Large, who had pitched against Betts in summer ball back in Nashville, Tennessee. Large had been sitting with his sister Lindsey, who called the home run. "She said right before the at-bat, 'He's about to hit a home run,'" Chris told *ESPNBoston.com*. "I said, 'What if I caught it?'" After the game, Chris, who faced Mookie when he was a 17-year-old at Overton High, was pleased to present the ball to his former adversary. "He told me he threw a 4-hitter against my team and I had two of the hits," says Mookie.[111] The ball was quickly passed along to Mookie's then-fiancée Brianna for safe keeping. Brianna and Mookie had known each other since they were classmates at Nashville's William Henry Oliver Middle School.[112]

He remained with the Red Sox through June 13, but was shuttled to Pawtucket for the rest of July, returning to Boston for good on August 1. For the PawSox, he played in 45 games, all but six in the outfield, and batted .355 (.417 OBP). In the 52 games he played for Boston, he hit .291 with five home runs and 18 RBIs. His on-base percentage was .368. Still only 21 years-old, his first grand slam came on August 29 in Tampa Bay against Rays ace Chris Archer. Once again he sought the advice of veterans and found a mentor in veteran Jonny Gomes, who schooled him about the repertoires of major-league pitchers and what to expect from them. Betts played 25 games in center field, 12 in right field, and 14 games at second base after Dustin Pedroia underwent season-ending surgery in September.

Mookie's first year was now history. Ever the perfectionist, he was his own worst critic. He analyzed his season and found himself wanting in several areas of the game. He had made too many base-running mistakes, swung at too many bad pitches, and he was still adjusting to outfield play. He vowed to learn and to improve. The admonition that he learned from his parents years earlier was to become his baseball mantra as well: "Somebody should only have to tell you once."

•

The Emergence of a Five-Tool Player (2015)

In 2015 it was obvious by the third inning of Opening Day (April 13) that Mookie was developing into a five-tool player who could hit with power, throw with distance and accuracy, play the field smoothly, and run the bases with skill and speed. The Red Sox were playing the Washington Nationals. Playing center field in the top of the first he committed grand larceny, soaring above the bullpen fence and robbing Bryce Harper of a sure homer. The baserunning part of the toolbox was on full display in the bottom of the first when he pulled off the rare double-steal-by-one-person-on-a-single-pitch trick.

With David Ortiz at the plate, Mookie was on first courtesy of a walk by Nationals starter Jordan Zimmermann. He timed the pitcher's delivery and took off for second, just beating the throw from the catcher. As he popped up out of his slide, he glanced toward third and saw that no one was covering the base so he took off again, leaving the helpless shortstop holding the ball. By the time third baseman Ryan Zimmerman received the throw and ran back to his base, Betts was able to slide in just before the tag. The Nats challenged both safe calls—at second and third—but after a lengthy pause, Betts was declared safe at both bases. Two stolen bases on one play. He later scored on a Big Papi hit.

The home opener had become the Mookie Betts Show. Two stolen bases and a stolen homer. He topped off the crime wave in the third by stealing the hearts of the Fenway faithful, blasting a three-run home run off Zimmermann that sailed over the Green Monster. The homer made him the third-youngest Red Sox player to go deep in an opening day game.

At the plate, Mookie was still struggling, especially when it came to laying off the breaking balls. Mookie didn't panic. He knew he was doing the little things that win ballgames: at the plate he was moving the runner over and pushing across a run. Once on base, he was going from first to third on hits; in the field he was keeping the double play in order and throwing to the right base. And then on June 12 he collided with the center-field wall at Fenway and missed the next couple of games. At that point he was batting an anemic .237 with only a .296 on-base percentage. Instead of sulking, he took the time to pick the brains of his more experienced teammates and he couldn't have chosen better mentors in Dustin Pedroia, David Ortiz, and Shane Victorino. When he returned to the lineup it was with renewed confidence. He began to hit with authority, finishing his sophomore campaign with a highly respectable .291 batting average and 18 homers.

On September 25, 2015, Rich Hill was pitching a two-hit gem for the Red Sox when Baltimore Orioles slugger Chris Davis hit a ball to the deepest reaches of Fenway. With total concentration, Mookie tracked it down, leaped high above the low bullpen wall, and snagged it for the final out of the 7–0 shutout.

As the 2015 season entered its final stages, the man who was drafted to play second base was moved to right field, where he would play half of his games at Fenway Park, considered one of the toughest defensive assignments in the major leagues. In hindsight, it's fair to say that the transition has worked out rather well. After all, if Mookie can solve a Rubik's Cube in under two minutes (and he can), surely Fenway's puzzling parameters could be conquered as well. In 2016, after only one full year patrolling this treacherous piece of real estate, he captured his first American League Gold Glove. At 24, he became the youngest Red Sox player since Fred Lynn (1975) to win the award.

At the plate, Mookie had 77 RBIs, 92 runs scored, and 21 stolen bases.

A Preview of Things to Come (2016)

Betts was in the Red Sox starting lineup on Opening Day 2016 in Philadelphia and homered in his second at-bat. That year also proved to be Betts's breakout year offensively, earning him selection to his first AL All-Star team and a second-place finish in the MVP voting. He also reached the coveted 200-hit plateau with 214, second-best in the junior circuit. The right fielder was at or near the top in an assortment of offensive categories. He maintained a .318 batting average while ringing up a league-high 672 at-bats and led the AL in total bases with 359. He finished second in runs scored (122), beat out 42 doubles, and hit 31 homers while driving in 113 runs. Once on the basepaths he continued to be a threat, stealing 26 bases and rattling the nerves of pitchers throughout the league. His on-base percentage was .363 and his slugging percentage a lofty .534.

Baltimore Orioles pitchers can be forgiven if they develop nervous tics and flashbacks whenever Mookie's name is mentioned. In 2016, he dismantled the Orioles pitching staff. In 79 at-bats, he sprayed 32 hits for a hearty .405 batting average. He scored 25 runs, nine of them via the long ball, and collected 22 RBIs. His on-base percentage was .472 and he slugged at a .810 clip, giving him an OPS of 1.282.

Baltimore fans were equally shell-shocked because Mookie did most of his damage in their own house at Camden Yards. In 37 at-bats at Orioles Park he hit eight homers, drove in 15 runs, and compiled a .514 batting average. His on-base percentage was an otherworldly .609 and his slugging percentage a jaw-dropping 1.162, giving him an OPs of 1.771. He also scored 18 times. At one point he had seven homers and 13 RBIs in 16 at-bats, an offensive display seldom seen even in the city that gave us Babe Ruth.

Now acknowledged as one of the best right fielders in the game, Mookie was kind enough to save some of his most memorable exploits for the hometown crowds at Fenway Park. Right field at baseball's oldest ballpark was earning the reputation as a killing ground where base hits were turned into outs and home runs often died at the wall. But Mookie also shone on the road. At the legendary home of the Bronx Bombers in September of 2016, the Red Sox were going for their 12th consecutive win. Chase Headley hit a line drive in Mookie's direction. He lost sight of it in the Yankee Stadium lights and started to slide too early. Somehow, he defied the laws of physics and caught it from the prone position. As if that weren't enough, he got to his feet and pegged the ball to first to double up Starlin Castro.

After Betts's 2016 season—which he completed with a 9.3 WAR second only to Mike Trout's 10.5—David Ortiz said about Betts: "He's not even as good as he's going to be when he gets more experience."[113]

In 2016, he did win that first Gold Glove—the first of three years in a row for him. Betts had only one error all season long and his strong, accurate arm produced 14 assists. He topped the major leagues in defensive runs saved with 32.

He came in second in MVP voting to Mike Trout, receiving a total of 311 points to Trout's 356. Betts, and not Trout, was the only player in the league to finish in the top three of every ballot cast, but Trout's 19 first-place votes outweighed Betts's nine.[114]

The Calm Before the Storm (2017)

It meant a lot to him to have ranked so highly. In early 2017, Betts said, "It's different for me this year just knowing in the back of my mind that I can do it, and don't need to force it. When you try to force things and do too much, bad things happen. I tell myself that I can do it. I can play at that level. It wasn't me going out and trying to do anything out of the ordinary. It just came from me just being Mookie."

He added, "I've learned to accept that I'm a role model to some people. I embrace it. I try to be the best I can be, smile, have fun playing the game, and make little aspects of the game enjoyable. That way, younger kids can go out, love playing the game, do things to have fun. . . . Even if it's a 2–2 game in the ninth inning, I want to have the same smile on my face that I had in the first inning. You don't want to get tight. You want to have fun and enjoy it. I think that's what's going to help me be the best I can be, help my guys be the best they can be, and young kids can see that, how to use that too . . . I think the challenge this year and going forward is going to be to continue being Mookie and not trying to be someone else."[115]

It was a big year for the Red Sox. Coming out of the doldrums, which had seen them suffer last-pace finishes in the AL East in 2012, 2014, and 2015 (there was a pleasant interlude in 2013 when they won a world championship), the Red Sox had finished first in 2016, four games ahead of the Orioles. In 2017, they finished first again, with an identical 93–69 record, this time two games ahead of the second-place Yankees.

In 2016, the Sox had been swept in the Division Series by the Cleveland Indians. In 2017, they managed one win in the ALDS, but it was against the ultimate world champion Houston Astros, so there was perhaps less shame there. Probably no one predicted the heights that Boston was going to achieve in 2018.

During the 2017 campaign, Mookie started off strongly. He frequently put the bat on the ball or he worked walks. He kept trying to get on base. From September 12, 2016 to April 19, 2017, he went 128 plate appearances without a strikeout. He hit. 293 in April, and .296 in June, but he struggled in the other months, only to rebound with a .281 mark in September.

In 2017, his batting average dipped to .264 and his home run total dropped from 31 to 24, but he added another 26 steals and drove in more than a hundred runs for the second straight year (102). His overall numbers and sublime defense were enough to elevate him to sixth place in the MVP balloting. He won his second consecutive Gold Glove and second consecutive Silver Slugger.

The Signature Year, To Date (2018)

Then came 2018, after which a shocking amount of bold print appeared in his Baseball-Reference batting stats. The dark ink indicated domination in categories that define superstardom. Aside from his league-leading runs scored (129) and batting average

(.346), he posted a Williamsesque .640 slugging percentage, and an on-base percentage plus slugging (OPS) figure in the rarefied Ruthian range, at 1.078. All this added up to a Most Valuable Player Award, and the voting wasn't close. He got all but two of the first-place votes and finished with 410 vote points, 145 points ahead of the runner-up, Angels outfielder Mike Trout.

The Gold Glove was his third in a row, putting him on track to equal Dewey Evans's collection of eight in 2023. Writer Alex Speier gave some of the credit to the Red Sox analytics folks: "On June 21, Twins first baseman Joe Mauer lined a ball to right-center field, ordinarily a hit or at least a ball that would have required a significant run to intercept it. But Betts stood in the path of the ball, barely moving in order to track it. After he fired the ball back into the infield, Betts grinned at the dugout and pulled a card from his back pocket, waving it triumphantly. A new defensive alignment that had been suggested by the Red Sox analytics department—and printed on a small card for the outfielders to check—had been spot on."[116]

Beside the MVP and Gold Glove, other hard-won hardware included a Silver Slugger Award, the AL batting title (the Rod Carew American League Batting Champion) trophy, and a World Series ring, making him the only player in history to capture all five in the same season.

Topping any award was the arrival of a beautiful baby daughter, Kynlee Ivory Betts, born to Mookie and Brianna Hammonds just nine days after the Red Sox clinched the World Series. Kynlee qualifies as baseball royalty, fitting since Mookie is a distant relative of Meghan Markle, Duchess of Sussex and wife of Britain's Prince Harry. Mookie may never have worn a royal crown but then Harry has never won a batting crown either.

There are many reasons for Mookie's career season in 2018. He has always let his bat and glove do much of the talking, but he is a world-class listener. Not since a young Ted Williams interrogated his teammates, coaches, and opponents about hitting, has a player so actively sought out and heeded the advice of veterans. Ted, who often drove veteran players to distraction with his questions about hitting and opposing pitchers, was particularly keen to get an edge on the game. When he first came up to the majors in 2014 for a one-week cup of coffee, Mookie learned about major-league pitchers from veteran Jonny Gomes. His quest for knowledge has continued unabated. His long list of "instructors" includes Dustin Pedroia and anyone else who is successful with the bat. In David Ortiz's final major-league seasons, Mookie used every opportunity to learn from one of the smartest hitters in the history of the game. In 2018, he was often seen in the dugout, post at-bat, analyzing what just happened with hitting coach Tim Hyers.

He worked hard, he prepared hard, and he played hard. But there was one factor that should be recognized: J. D. Martinez. The Red Sox signed Martinez in 2018, with the goal of filling the vacuum left by David "Big Papi" Ortiz. Although there will never be another Big Papi, Martinez did everything expected of him and more. At the plate, he confirmed and enhanced his reputation as one of the most feared hitters in the game. He scored 111 runs, accumulated 188 hits, batted at a lofty .330 clip, and stroked 43 homers. He led the American League in RBIs with 130 and in total bases with 358. His OBP was .402 and his slugging percentage .629 (1.031 OPS). He joined Mookie on the All-Star team and finished fourth in the MVP voting. He made a legitimate bid for the Triple Crown. He won *two* Silver Sluggers—one as DH and one as an outfielder. No other player has ever done so. So which was J. D.'s biggest contribution to the Red Sox season? Arguably it was the advice he gave to his teammates, most prominently Mookie Betts.

Mookie has cited Martinez for his generous sharing of hitting tips. It's hardly surprising that the two have become great friends. They have developed a mutual admiration society and it has paid huge dividends. One is an unselfish guru of hitting and the other is a great listener. Mookie soaks up hitting advice like a sponge, retains it, and incorporates it into his plate strategy. He has openly credited J. D. for a rebound season in which he raised his batting average by 82 points (from .264 to a league-best .346) and his home run production by eight (from 24 in 2017 to 32 in 2018). This was accomplished despite the fact that Betts played in 17 fewer games and had 108 fewer at-bats.

In midseason, David Ortiz said, "He has such special talent. I'm not surprised what he's doing. To me, to be honest with you, he's going to get better. That's how Mookie is—Mookie is always hungry. This guy, even when he's doing well, he wants to do better. That's the kid I saw coming up with us."[117]

Fred Lynn agrees. "At the plate, Mookie has displayed unbelievable power for a guy his size. He's up there and he attacks. He's not up there to walk; he's up there to attack the ball. That first pitch coming—he's swinging. He's slashing. Looking at it right now, Mookie has displayed an ability to hit—at .346—that's hitting." Indeed, over the course of his career, swinging at the first pitch he sees, Betts is batting .312.

Red Sox hitting coach Tim Hyers enthused over one overlooked aspect of Mookie's year at the plate:

"He hit .300 with two strikes! That's *incredible*! In round numbers, if you hit .200 with two strikes, we look at that as above average. I think the average in 2017 was probably .165, .175, something like that. That was like the average in Major League Baseball with two strikes. If a player's hitting .200 with two strikes, that's well above average and we're happy. That's a number that's going to help you out. Mookie hit .300 this year.

"[As] a major-league player, over 50 percent of your at-bats are going to be with two strikes. A lot of players overlook that. It's not something they want to deal with, because two strikes is the pitcher's advantage, but you're going to be in that position a lot in your career so we always say, 'You better have a plan.' You better develop a plan for that, because a lot of your season's going to be with two strikes. Then Mookie goes and hits .300 with two strikes. That just tells you that, in one of the most difficult situations—we call that advantage to the pitcher—and he's still hitting .300."

Hyers, who has seen and coached a lot of hitters in his career, has a special appreciation of Betts's batting eye.

"From day one, he's one of the most impressive hitters I've ever been around, at identifying pitches early. Seeing the ball real early out of the hand. Understanding the strike zone. Picks up spin. Sees strikes out of the hand. Early recognition that really allows him . . . he's ultra-quick. Very athletic. Great hand-eye coordination. If you put all the other stuff together, it's something."

Mookie's batting average really dipped in 2017, down from .318 in 2016 to .264. Then he leapt all the way up to .346 in 2018. Which of course begs the question, what was the cause of what seemed to be a dramatic dip in 2017?

"The league adjusts to you as a player. They try to find weaknesses and holes, and I think he always swung quick and had a flat swing plane. It works. There's nothing wrong with it. He came into the league and he did really well, but I think in '17 they [pitchers] started throwing him a lot more sliders. Pitches with depth, we call it. Balls that break down. Batters with flatter swing planes, they try to work on the barrel. I think maybe he created a little bad habit of staying too steep and chasing some of the breaking balls running away from righties. I think he kind of lost some posture, lost some mechanics that I was sworn to reintroduce and talk to him about when I came over here in '18. We talked about just getting on plane with that pitch. I want to say that they threw him almost 200 more sliders in '17 than they did in '16. That was just to get him off-balance and to keep him out of the air.

"We made a few adjustments with his swing this year. We just talked about getting a better base, synching his upper body and lower body, but the big thing was to get on plane and add a little bit of depth on the back side of his swing plane to match the arc of some of those pitches, especially down in the zone. It was only a thing just to remind him of who he was and things that he did. Just adding a few cosmetic things.

"He's just a quick learner. Also, we had J. D. with us. He's really a student of hitting and mechanics. He picked up on a lot of little things like that, how they were pitching him. I think that was the big reason we saw the jump in the power, because they tried to go at him again, down in the zone with some of those pitches, and he just was ready for them and capitalized early.

"They were just, 'Whoa, we've got to make another adjustment on this guy. He's killing us. He's a different guy from '17 to '18.'

"I don't call it a major change. I just call it a cosmetic change in a couple of things, but you could talk to him about it. But it was a difference in getting on plane, we call it, just getting on plane with that pitch to match the arc, to avoid that rollover, the routine ground balls. He hit line drives and got the ball in the air just a little bit more. I think that helped him hit some homers."

Betts's ability to adapt and adjust extends to defense as well. His quickness and superior footwork allows manager Alex Cora to use him at different positions when the situation calls for it. Last season that even included a stint in the infield.

Betts, the former second baseman, got the opportunity to play second base for part of the August 3, 2018 game against the Yankees. "It was like a dream come true," he said after the game. Haven't been there since 2014. That's why I take my ground balls, just in case."[118]

In the World Series, he said he'd be glad to play second base, thereby enabling J. D. Martinez to play the outfield so that the Sox wouldn't lose their regular DH's bat at Dodger Stadium. "If that's what it takes to win, I'll do whatever. Gotta do anything to get that ring."[119]

A Tribute to MLB

(with apologies to Gilbert and Sullivan and the *Pirates of Penzance*)

He is the very model of a modern major-leaguer-er
He catches balls hit to the walls and often even further-er
He knows the angles of the park, and plays the ball accordingly
A master of right field in Fenway's strange geometry

He's well acquainted with the zone, and all matters bat-alogical
He hits the pitch to left and right and sometimes to the Triangle
He dives, he hits, he steals, he throws; his talent is incredible
He does it all, game after game, and with a smile angelical

Some Red Sox players from the past are completely unforgettable
Like Papi, Rice, Ted, and Yaz– to list them alphabetical
To that group, we'll add a name that's not the least heretical
'Cause Mookie Betts possesses skills beyond the theoretical

Who knows what this man's future holds? The question is rhetorical
His numbers when it's over will no doubt be historical
Someday we'll look back in time to when he was a rookie
We'll smile at all the things he's done and thank the gods for Mookie

The Bling

There's another possible reason for Mookie's MVP performance in 2018 and it was on display for all to see whenever he entered the batter's box. Even before Mookie signed his new $20 million contract for 2019, his $10,500,000 paycheck for 2018 meant he could afford some pretty decent jewelry. But Mookie was never the showy type. The only bling that he wore was a gold necklace that his father had given him in high school.

In March of 2018, he added a second fashion accessory, although it was more thing than bling. It was a small plastic ball and bat, attached by string and dangling around his neck. The bauble was given to him at a spring training game in West Palm Beach, Florida, where the Red Sox were playing a spring training game with the Houston Astros. The boy who gave him the trinket was 12-year-old Griffin Cantrell from Paducah, Kentucky. Mookie was the young boy's hero and he wanted to show him how much he appreciated him. "Everyone asks for different things from players," explained his father, Matt Cantrell. "He thought it would be cool if he could give him something for taking time out to stop."[120]

Mookie accepted the gift, gave Griffin an autographed ball, and posed for a picture with him. "It was really cool," recalled Griffin. End of story. Well, not quite. Mookie took a genuine liking to the necklace and wore it almost continuously. Coincidentally—or otherwise—he also began the season with an offensive barrage. In April he batted .367 with eight homers and 18 RBIs. His slugging percentage was .797 and his on-base percentage was .457, giving him an OPS of 1.240. He continued his rampage in May, adding nine more homers and 19 RBIs while batting .372 for the month. An injury slowed him temporarily in late May and he missed 13 games, but when he returned, he gradually regained his stroke and the relentless assault on American League pitchers continued.

As the season wore on, people began to notice the new adornment and the way Mookie carefully arranged it during each at-bat. He was asked about it but couldn't recall its source, so he put out a special appeal on WEEI for the secret giver to come forward. The mystery was solved when Griffin reminded Mookie of their brief spring training exchange.

Against all odds, the necklace somehow withstood the rigors of a major-league season—the swings, the brushback pitches, the diving catches, the head-first slides into second. Even Lloyd's of London would have hesitated at insuring such a fragile objet d'art. In October, the good luck charm was still intact. Mookie also wore it as part of his everyday attire—to social occasions, and while relaxing at home. It had become part of him. "I just don't take it off," he told WEEI's Bob Bradford. "There's no way it's going to break. I only take it off if I get my neck worked on, but other than that I don't take it off."

It received maximum national and international exposure during the World Series. When the Red Sox emerged victorious, Betts wasn't ready to attribute any supernatural powers to the trinket. "It's not necessarily a good-luck charm," he claimed. "I just like it."[121]

Traditionally, World Series champions are presented with rings and each year they seem to become larger and more ostentatious. Mookie's ring will no doubt clash with his plastic necklace, but at the end of his career the ring—or rings—and the plastic necklace will no doubt have an equal place of honor in the Betts household. Who knows, he may even wear it to his Hall of Fame induction ceremony someday.

Giving Back

League and World Series championships aside, there were two postseason accomplishments by Betts that didn't make the record books but that say a lot about the man. There was no sellout crowd to acknowledge it, but it revealed the real Mookie, the man behind the uniform. It took place late at night outside the Boston Public Library just hours after the Red Sox had tied the World Series at one game apiece with a 4–2 victory over the LA Dodgers at Fenway, a win in which Mookie had gone 3-for-4 and scored a run. If not for former Red Sox utilityman Lou Merloni, the incident might have gone completely unnoticed, but Merloni, now a WEEI radio personality, found out about it and spread the news. Betts and his cousin had been seen distributing hot meals of steak tips and chicken to dozens of homeless people outside the library. It was a cold night and they wore hoodies that kept out the chill and also served to make them anonymous. Some revelers passed by unaware of the identities of these two men supplying the meals. Most were gathered in cozy bars or at home with family to celebrate the win.

When the good deed made the news, Betts was genuinely surprised by all the fuss. Where he came from, people helped people, simple as that. When asked about it before Game Three at Dodger Stadium in Los Angeles, he shrugged. "I've been blessed with everything I have, and I might as well share it," he said.

By December, much of the revelry had died down and the banquet season was in full swing. Before the offseason was over, there would be countless dinners and endless speeches where praise would flow like cheap wine. But Mookie was more concerned about giving back. Just days before Christmas, he presented brand-new bikes to a group of Nashville children. "You always remember your first bike," explained Mookie. And when that bike is given to you by the American League MVP, it's especially unforgettable. "It's amazing just to know that you're making somebody happy in some way," Betts told Hayden Bird of *Boston.com*. "I just know that to see kids smiling and enjoying it makes me happy. I'm fortunate to be where I am and [I] just definitely want to spread the blessings."[122]

Another way Mookie pays it forward is to help city kids in Boston and Nashville get a fair shot at their own baseball dreams. "With baseball, I know there are a lot of kids who want to play ball, who are good enough to play ball and just don't have that opportunity. I'm trying to do my best to make it happen." Usually Mookie's acts of charity are done in a behind-the-scenes, low-key manner. He has raised money for those unable to pay their medical bills and surgeries. "I just try to help where I can," he told the *Tennessean*. "I was blessed with opportunities to succeed, so I've got to pass it down to the next person." Little wonder he was named Tennessean Sportsperson of the Year. "Dreams have come true," he added.[123]

On December 22, 2018, before a Tennessee Titans home football game against the Washington Redskins, Mookie was honored as the "12th Titan." Part of that ceremony involves plunging the Titans' sword into the ground. He was told that in 2016, Nashville Predators hockey star P. K. Subban had doused himself in water before sticking the sword into the turf then ripping off his shirt and letting loose with a scream that echoed throughout Nissan Stadium.

"Yeah," the quiet hero said. "I'm not doing that."

During celebrations that followed the Red Sox' 2018 World Series-clinching game, reliever Joe Kelly was in the midst of an interview when his two-year-old son, Knox, shouted "Mookie Betts" into the microphone. This is how an entire continent of baseball fans learned that the charming young man was a Mookie fan.

His father was dealt to the LA Dodgers in the offseason, but Knox wasn't about to change his allegiance to the Mookster. He'd been mixing with the Dodgers players during 2019 spring training sessions and afterwards, in the middle of the crowded clubhouse, manager Dave Roberts asked him what his favorite team was, hoping to hear it was the Dodgers. Kids, after all, can be fickle, attaching themselves to people and things that are nearest to hand.

Knox didn't hesitate. His answer was "Mookie Betts." So not only is Mookie an MVP, he's a one-man team.[124]

Mookie at the Plate

Ted Williams would have loved Mookie Betts. He would have loved his intelligence, his patience, his compact swing, his bat speed, his quickness, his hand-eye coordination. He would have loved his desire to improve, his curiosity, his habit of asking questions and listening to the answers. He would have applauded his combination of power and average, his willingness to take a base on balls. He would have placed him in the company of Mays or Aaron, always with the caution that he must do it consistently over a long period. Ted would have asked him a hundred questions and Mookie would not only have known the answers but would have asked Ted another hundred of his own.

In *Ted Williams' Hit List*, Williams went through hundreds of candidates before settling on the ones that fit his criteria of great hitters. Those criteria could have been written using Mookie as the prototypical Williams-style hitter.

Ted was like a little kid when he started talking about young hitters and often became animated, gripping an imaginary bat and looking out at some pitcher that had suddenly inhabited his mind's eye. He did, however, have a definite bias towards players who could hit for power and average.

Ted left Pete Rose out of his book, as well as Wade Boggs, George Brett, and other hitters that many place among the all-time greats. At one point, he quoted his friend Mickey Mantle on the subject of Rose, saying, "If I hit like Rose, I'd wear a dress." He also said that Dewey Evans's stance made him "want to throw up."

Would Mookie Betts be on Ted Williams's Hit List if Ted were around to see him? There's no question about it, although Ted would no doubt have cautioned that he has to perform at or near the same high level throughout his career. In the meantime, he would have put him number one on his personal on-deck circle and would have followed his career path with rapt interest.

Mookie's Game-Winning Hits

Mookie Betts only had one game-winning hit in his first year with the Red Sox. He played in 52 games, drove in 18 runs, and scored 34. He made a splash. He contributed. He helped win games for the team, but he just had the one game-winner. It came, thanks to a grand slam. Plenty more followed—10 of them in 2015 and 14 the year after that.

August 29, 2014: It was a tough outing for Tampa Bay's Chris Archer. He gave up three runs in the top of the first inning. The Sox had two outs and a baserunner in the second inning when an RBI double brought in a fourth Boston run. A walk and a hit batter loaded the bases. Bang! Betts hit a grand slam to left field. That made it 8–0, Red Sox. They didn't score any more, but the Rays put up four as the game wore on. That made Mookie's blast stand as the hit that won the game.

April 10, 2015: More than 41,000 packed into Yankee Stadium for a Friday night game. It started at 7:08 p.m., but at 1:08 a.m., the game was still on. Boston had a 3–0 lead in the sixth, but New York scored two in the bottom of the sixth, and then tied it up in the ninth. David Ortiz hit a solo home run in the top of the 16th, but Mark Teixeira matched it with a homer of his own in the bottom of the inning. The game wore on. In the top of the 19th, Xander Bogaerts singled, stole second, and advanced to third on a passed ball. There was one out. Betts was 1-for-8 in the game. And he made another out, but he made it count—he hit a sacrifice fly to deep center field. Bogaerts tagged up and Boston took and held the lead. Red Sox 6, Yankees 5, in 19 innings.

April 27, 2015: A walk-off single. Joe Kelly started for the Red Sox, and gave up five runs in six innings, three in the first and one run each in the third and fourth. Thanks to Pablo Sandoval, the Sox scored twice in the first and again in the fourth. They added another in the fifth, and then tied it in the eighth when Mookie singled, moved up on a single and again on a wild pitch, and then scored the tying run on a sac fly. In the bottom of the ninth, a strikeout and two singles put Red Sox runners on first and second. Betts came up to bat. The first pitch was wild, and both baserunners moved up. The second pitch was struck, for a single to center field. Game over.

May 5, 2015: Neither team scored for the first five innings. In fact, Tampa Bay's Drew Smyly hadn't allowed a hit. In the bottom of the sixth, Mookie Betts hit Smyly's second pitch off the SPORTS AUTHORITY sign above Fenway Park's Green Monster. There was only one more run in the game, for either side—Mookie Betts hit the first pitch of the eighth inning out, into the second row of the Monster seats. 2–0, Red Sox.

May 14, 2015: In the top of the fourth, Shane Victorino homered for one Red Sox run in Seattle. The Mariners moved a runner station to station and tied it up in the bottom of the sixth. Fernando Rodney came in to try and hold the Sox in the ninth, but Brock Holt doubled and Bogaerts sacrificed him to third. Mookie Betts came up and battled for six pitches, fouling off three consecutive two-strike pitches. On the seventh pitch, he hit a ball deep enough to left field for a sacrifice fly. As it happens, the left fielder dropped the ball so Betts reached base, but the Brockstar was the only one to score. It was enough.

June 21, 2015: The Red Sox racked up 13 runs before the Royals finally scored two in the bottom of the ninth. Two solo home runs (by Hanley Ramirez and David Ortiz) accounted for the first two runs. The third, decisive run scored in the top of the fifth—a two-run homer by Mookie Betts, with Sandy Leon on base. Bogaerts cleared the bases with a double later in the inning, but those runs were all gravy, as it turns out. Mookie had a double, a triple, and a homer in the game. All he needed for a cycle was a single, but it was not to be.

July 4, 2015: The Red Sox hosted Houston at Fenway Park on Independence Day. The Astros were comfortably in first in the AL West; the Red Sox were last in the AL East. Boston's Clay

Buchholz, though, pitched a complete-game masterpiece, allowing just one measly run in the top of the ninth. Bogaerts drove in Betts with the first Boston run in the first. Betts hit a sacrifice fly to drive in Shane Victorino in the second. The Red Sox added on four more as the game progressed, two of them runs Betts drove in.

July 11, 2015: One week later, still at Fenway, the Sox hosted the Yankees. Alex Rodriguez put the Yankees on the board with a solo home run in the top of the first. By the bottom of the seventh, it was 3–2, Red Sox. With two outs and a runner on second, Mookie greeted reliever Adam Warren with a triple to right-center, over the head of right fielder Chris Young, giving the Red Sox the run that made the margin of difference and won the game.

August 18, 2015: It was 7–0, Red Sox, before the visiting Indians scored their only run of the game. The Red Sox had the bases loaded with one out in the bottom of the second. Mookie Betts saw strike one from Trevor Bauer, strike two, and then seemed to have struck out on the third pitch. He started walking back to the Boston dugout, but was told, no, he'd fouled it off. He was fine with that and then hit a bases-loaded triple over the head of Francisco Lindor. The Red Sox won, 9–1.

August 21, 2015: Blake Swihart doubled in two runs in the bottom of the second inning. After a Josh Rutledge single allowed Swihart to go to third, Mookie singled to left field to score him. It was Red Sox 3, Royals 0 after two. Betts singled Swihart in again in the bottom of the fourth, but Kansas City only scored two runs in the game, so his second-inning single was the one that won the game.

September 7, 2015: The Jays scored once in the top of the first. The Sox scored once in the bottom of the second, twice in the bottom of the third, and twice more in the bottom of the fourth. It was a weak single to third base that drove in that fifth run. With a final score of 11–4, that one won the game. Mookie was 3-for-5 in the game, riding a 13-game hitting streak.

April 15, 2016: The Red Sox got three in the first inning. In the second inning, Christian Vázquez doubled off Fenway's left-field wall. He moved up 90 feet on a groundout by Jackie Bradley Jr., and scored on Betts's single to left. That made it 4–1, Boston. The Sox beat the Blue Jays, 5–3.

April 20, 2016: Bogaerts drove in one and Ortiz drove in two as the Sox took a 3–0 lead in the first. In the bottom of the second, Betts came up to bat with Bradley on second base. Betts, coming out of a 2-for-21 slump, hit a pitch from Chris Archer out of the park. Boston 5, Tampa Bay 0. The final was 7–3.

April 22, 2016: Two days later, with a 4-for-5 night in Houston, he was 8-for-14 over three games. He won this one, too, with a double to left field in the top of the second which scored Bradley. Betts scored on a wild pitch later in the game. The Astros went down, 6–2.

April 30, 2016: On the last day of April, the Red Sox were home again, and the New York Yankees were in town. Rick Porcello threw seven shutout innings and turned the ball over to a pair of relievers who kept the New Yorkers scoreless. All it took was one Red Sox run to win the game (though they enjoyed themselves, scoring eight times). That first run (and the second one, too), scored on a double by Mookie Betts in the bottom of the second inning.

May 15, 2016: With 19 runs total in a 10–9 game, it was—of course—the 10th run that beat the Astros. The RBI star of the game was Sox catcher Ryan Hanigan with four, and it was he who singled in the ninth run. Then it was Mookie Betts who tripled in Hanigan with the 10th. A few days later, Betts had five RBIs in a 9–1 victory over Cleveland. But not one of them was the game-winner.

May 24, 2016: Again, it was a sacrifice fly that earned Betts credit for a game-winning drive. The Rockies were at Fenway, and the run Betts drove in (Christian Vázquez, who tagged and scored in the second inning) was the fourth run in an 8–3 Red Sox win.

May 31, 2016: At Camden Yards, Mookie Betts hit a lead-off homer for the Red Sox off Baltimore starter Kevin Gausman. Dustin Pedroia, batting second, hit a homer, too. In the top of the second, with two outs and two on, Betts again faced Gausman. He homered again. He drove in five of the six Red Sox runs, and his second homer was the game-winner.

June 19, 2016: David Price allowed the Mariners just one run at this game in Boston, a home run by Franklin Gutierrez. The Red Sox tied it in the sixth, and then Betts homered to lead off the seventh off reliever Edwin Diaz. The final score: 2–1.

July 20, 2016: The Red Sox used six pitchers, but they beat the visiting San Francisco Giants, 11–7. The eighth Red Sox run was the last one scored in the bottom of the second, coming via a double by Betts, the fifth extra-base hit of the inning.

July 29, 2016: The Red Sox were playing the Los Angeles Angels at Angel Stadium of Anaheim. The 6–2 complete-game win by Rick Porcello upped his record to 14–2. The game-winner was a sacrifice fly in the top of the fourth off Tim Lincecum.

August 1, 2016: Safeco Field, Seattle. Sox starter Eduardo Rodriguez worked 6 ⅓ innings, only allowing one run. But the Red Sox had none. Finally, the Sox tied it with a solo home run by Aaron Hill in the top of the eighth. Leading off the ninth was Mookie Betts, who homered to win the game.

August 13, 2016: After Boston scored once in the third, the Diamondbacks scored twice in the fourth and once more in the fifth. In the bottom of the fifth, Leon homered for the Red Sox, before Benintendi drove in a run. Then Betts squirted a single between shortstop and third base, and the Red Sox took the lead. They didn't give it up and scored twice more in the sixth.

The very next day—August 14—Mookie Betts had perhaps his biggest day on offense. He homered three times and drove in eight runs, as the Red Sox beat Arizona, 16–2. It was, however, Andrew Benintendi who gets credit for the game-winner.

April 17, 2017: Tampa Bay got two runs off Steven Wright in the top of the first. Hanley Ramirez got one run back for the Red Sox in the bottom of the inning. In the bottom of the second, Benintendi drove in a pair and then Mookie singled in one. That made it 4–2. The Rays scored another run later in the game, but Wright got the win and Mookie made the difference.

April 20, 2017: Chris Sale worked eight, without allowing a run. The Red Sox failed to score, too. In the top of the ninth, Bogaerts knocked in one for Boston, but then Toronto's Kendrys Morales homered off Craig Kimbrel to tie it up, 1–1. Then, with the bases loaded, Mookie tripled. 4–1, and Kimbrel got the win.

April 23, 2017. The third Betts game-winner in a six-day stretch. The Red Sox had lost two in a row in Baltimore. They put up four runs in the top of the first, and that was enough to win this one, 6–2. Facing his old friend Kevin Gausman (see May 31, 2016), Betts hit a three-run homer to win the game. Eduardo Rodriguez allowed only one hit in six innings.

May 11, 2017: In Milwaukee, Boston got one in the top of the first. The Brewers got one in the bottom of the sixth. In the top of the ninth, with the two men on, Betts took a 2–2 pitch over the fence in left field. Kimbrel had already closed out the eighth. He struck out the side in the bottom of the ninth and booked another win.

June 16, 2017: Mookie Betts's leadoff homer to deep left field in the top of the eighth broke a 1–1 tie at Houston's Minute Maid Park. Drew Pomeranz had taken a three-hit shutout into the seventh, but with one pitch Brian McCann had tied the game. Will Harris relieved for the Astros. His first pitch was hit up and over the Crawford Boxes to give Boston a 2–1 lead, one that held.

July 2, 2017: First-inning RBI: Hanley Ramirez. Second-inning RBI: Mookie Betts singled, following Tzu-Wei Lin's triple. The Blue Jays scored once in the bottom of the second. Perhaps thinking the game was a little too tight, with just the one-run margin, Mookie added a three-run homer in the top of the fourth and then a two-run homer in the top of the sixth. Now it was Betts 6, Blue Jays 1. He singled in two more in the seventh. All told, it was Betts 8, the rest of the Red Sox 7, and the Blue Jays 1. Last August 14, he had eight RBIs but no game-winner. On this July afternoon, he drove in eight and would have had the game-winner even if the Jays had scored two, three, four, five, or six runs.

July 16, 2017: In Boston, it was a day-night doubleheader against the Yankees. The Red Sox lost the afternoon game, 3–0, despite being given seven bases on balls. They won the night game, 3–0. Starter Masahiro Tanaka was Mookie's victim, in the bottom of the third. Home run to left field. Two runs on the board. That was all it took.

August 16, 2017: Fenway Park patrons were a little despondent this Wednesday night when the St. Louis Cardinals scored four runs in the top of the second inning. The Sox got back two when pitcher Lance Lynn threw the ball away on a ground ball that Eduardo Nuñez hit back to the pitcher and saw a runner score from second. Then Betts hit a sac fly for the second run. In the bottom of the ninth, the 4–2 Cardinals lead was halved when Xander Bogaerts led off with a homer. A walk, a strikeout, and another walk put two on, but then Nuñez popped out foul to first base. Betts came to the rescue; on a 3–2 count, he doubled off the Monster, driving in two. Bradley had been off with the pitch and scored from first base, only because Yadier Molina had trouble corralling the relay, in the walk-off.

August 23, 2017: The four runs the Red Sox scored in the top of the ninth at Progressive Field sealed the 6–1 win, but it was Mookie Betts who drove in the second (and, therefore, winning) run of the game in the top of the eighth. Mitch Moreland had homered earlier. Edwin Encarnacion homered for Cleveland's only run.

September 16, 2017: It was another one of those games on September 12; Betts had six RBIs, but not the one that won the game. Four days later, he homered leading off the top of the second at Tropicana. In the sixth inning, Benintendi reached first after forcing out Vázquez at second base. Benny was balked to second, then stole third and scored easily when Betts singled to left. The Rays later scored once, but it was the second one Betts drove in that had won the game.

September 20, 2017: Chris Sale (eight innings) and Austin Maddox shut out the Orioles, 9–0, pleasing the Red Sox fans who had flocked into Camden Yards. In the top of the fourth, Benintendi singled and Betts homered to left. That's all it took to win, though Deven Marrero added a two-run homer later in the inning and Boston batters added five more during the course of the game.

April 25, 2018: Mookie Betts led off the game in Toronto with a home run to left field before the Blue Jays came back to tie it. In the top of the fifth, Brock Holt drove in one run, but in the bottom of the fifth, the Jays tied it. Then Yangervis Solarte hit a solo home run in the sixth to give Toronto a 3–2 lead. Holt got on base in the top of the seventh, and Betts hit a two-run homer to left to restore the Red Sox lead, now 4–3, which stood as the final score.

May 2, 2018: Just seven days later, Betts had another multi-homer game. The first was, again, a solo home run to lead off an inning, but this time it was the bottom of the fourth and it put a dent in the Royals' 3–0 lead. J. D. Martinez slammed a two-run homer later in the inning to tie it up. Mookie hit another solo home run in the fifth to give the Red Sox a 4–3 edge. And then he did it again in the seventh—another solo shot, all three off Danny Duffy—to make it 5–3, Boston. Since the Royals got one back in the top of the eighth, it was Betts's third home run that was the game-winner, 5–4.

May 22, 2018: A three-run Mookie homer in the top of the fifth inning turned out to be all the team needed to win, 4–2, at Tampa Bay. Rafael Devers provided a little extra insurance with a homer of his own in the sixth inning.

July 2, 2018: This was a game Rick Porcello will brag about for years. Playing in a National League park (Nationals Park in Washington), there was no DH and the pitcher had to bat. Following a single, a hit-by-pitch, and an intentional walk, three-time Cy Young Award winner Max Scherzer (2013, 2016, and 2017) had two outs and faced the opposing Red Sox pitcher, Porcello. What happened? Porcello tripled and cleared the bases. Porcello's hit didn't win the game for himself, though. He gave up a pair of solo home runs, and later saw Joe Kelly surrender another one. In the meantime, though, Mookie Betts hit a solo home run to lead off the seventh inning. Porcello did get the win, and bragging rights for his prowess with the bat.

July 12, 2018: With the fifth and final run in the bottom of the fourth inning, the Red Sox had accumulated enough runs to beat the Blue Jays, 6–4 for their 10th consecutive victory. Toronto had held a 2–0 lead since the first inning, but Sandy Leon knocked in the first Sox run of the big inning, and then—on the 13th pitch of a long at-bat—Mookie Betts hit a grand slam over everything in left field to plate four more. It was starter J. A. Happ's last pitch of the game.

July 27, 2018: The Twins took a 3–2 lead in the top of the ninth, but Devers led off the bottom of the ninth with a game-tying home run. In the 10th inning, Mookie Betts put one into the Monster seats for a walk-off win.

August 29, 2018: Those 11-run innings will more often than not win you the game. The Miami Marlins were in town and scored in the second, third, fifth, and seventh innings, for a total of five runs. The Sox had scored three times and were down by two. In the bottom of the seventh, they unloaded for 11 runs on 12 hits, without a home run. There was one Miami error and one intentional walk. Nuñez, Kinsler, Swihart, Bradley, and Betts each had two hits in the inning. Betts's first, a double, drove in the run that provided the margin of victory.

September 3, 2018: In the top of the fifth, in Atlanta, the Red Sox scored first. And second, and third. The runs batted in went to Kinsler, Vázquez, and Betts. The single to left field by Betts produced the third run in an 8–2 win.

September 24, 2018: The Red Sox had already clinched the AL East, but a team needs to keep winning games in order to stay sharp. In the bottom of the second inning, Baltimore's Dylan Bundy served up five base hits. Brock Holt and Vázquez each drove in one run, and then Mookie homered over the Monster to account for two more. The final was 6–2. It was Betts's 32nd home run of the season, a career high. It was the third game in a row he had homered.

Mookie's nine game-winning hits in 2018 help illustrate why almost no one tracks game-winners.

That season was also noteworthy for him for other reasons. He was an All-Star for the third time, won his third Gold Glove, his second Silver Slugger, and led the league in batting average, runs scored, and slugging. He won the Most Valuable Player award in the American League. What more could you ask for?

As was the case with JBJ and Benny, Mookie Betts—despite scoring 16 runs and driving in four—has not yet had a game-winning hit in postseason play.

Mookie at WAR

A reported 1,271 players appeared in one or more major-league games in 2018. The single player with the greatest Wins Above Replacement (WAR) was Mookie Betts. He was ranked at 10.9 WAR, the highest mark for any position player since the 11.8 recorded by Barry Bonds in 2002.

Chris Sale was at 6.9, J. D. Martinez 6.4, David Price 4.4, and Andrew Benintendi 3.9.

The only two players in Red Sox history to reach 10.9 in WAR were Ted Williams in 1946 (10.9) and Carl Yastrzemski in 1967 (12.5).

For the past four years (2015 through 2018), Betts has led the Red Sox in WAR.

The Boston Baseball Writers more or less concurred, voting him team MVP for three years running starting in 2016.

Combining Speed and Power

Betts is the only Red Sox player in team history to record 20 homers and 20 stolen bases for three seasons in a row. Only Jacoby Ellsbury (2011) and Mookie Betts (2018) have ever had 30-30 seasons.

Combining Batting Average and Power

Betts is the first Red Sox player since Ted Williams in 1957 to lead the major leagues in both batting average and slugging percentage.

Some Other Numbers on Offense

Through 2018, Betts has hit 89 homers as a leadoff hitter, far eclipsing Dom DiMaggio's 69 for the most in Red Sox history. Sixteen times he's homered as the first Boston batter in the game.

Both on April 17 and May 2, Betts hit three home runs in a game. As of the beginning of the 2019 season, he has four three-homer games, more than anyone in Red Sox history. No major leaguer has ever done this before turning 26 years old.

He's putting up some big numbers at an early age. He's had four 20-homer seasons before turning 26 years old. Only Ted Williams, Tony Conigliaro, and Jim Rice have done that for the Red Sox.

In 2016, he scored more than 100 runs for the third season in a row. Only one Red Sox player ever did that before age 26: The Kid, Ted Williams. Betts scored 129 runs in 2018—that's the most for any Red Sox player since Dom DiMaggio scored 131 in 1950.

Mookie is also a doubles machine. He hit 47 doubles in 2018, the fourth year in a row that he hit more than 40. The only other Red Sox player to do so four years in a row was Wade Boggs, who did it seven years in a row.

Speaking of the 40 doubles, and combining that with base stealing, Betts is the only player in major-league history to hit 40+ doubles *and* steal 20-plus bases in four consecutive seasons.

With 177 doubles since the start of his first full season (2015), he leads the majors in two-base hits.

He has been the leadoff batter in 461 of his 644 major-league games through the 2018 season. Batting leadoff sees a hitter start the game with no one on the bases, making it a little harder to collect runs batted in—though he has hit 20 first-inning home runs. He's a .307 hitter with a .373 on-base percentage batting first in the order.

Defense

Ballplayers have lot of superstitions and phobias. They usually involve not stepping on the base line while running on and off the field, or an irrational fear of batting against pitchers with surnames like Ryan, Koufax, or Martinez. Some phobias are stranger than others and have little to do with baseball. Mookie once revealed to Katie Nolan of *Garbage Time* on FS1 that he has a fear of rust.

"I hate rust, it messes me up. It makes my skin crawl. I have to get away from it. It's been this way pretty much my entire life. I don't know why I don't like it; if I see rust it just really messes me up." He added, "It makes my skin crawl. I can't sit right. I have to go and get away from it. I don't know why."

That's one good thing about Gold Gloves and Silver Slugger bats. They don't rust. Mookie now has three consecutive Gold Gloves as the best defensive right fielder in the American League and three consecutive Fielding Bible Awards as best defensive right field in the majors.

Fangraphs says he earned 83 defensive runs saved over the past three seasons (2016 to 2018)—the most runs saved by any fielder in any position in the majors.

One advantage he had is his speed afoot. This allows him, Fred Lynn notes, "to play a little bit more shallow and go back on balls and get them. You know, that kid can run. I've seen him play pretty shallow and dare guys to hit it over his head—and yet I've not seen them hit it over his head and keep it in the park. He snags those suckers. He has a pretty good idea of what's going on that particular day, the pitcher, the batter, and the game situation.

"Dwight [Evans] played a little bit deeper unless there was somebody in scoring position and then he'd cheat in a little bit so he could throw them out. For arm strength, it's Dwight. But in terms of foot speed, it's Mookie all day long. Mookie does have a good arm, don't get me wrong. He can throw; he gets his whole body into it."

One Very Special Game That Didn't Feel as Good as It Could Have

Whether it's through defense, hitting, or a combination thereof, winning the game is the name of the game. On August 9, 2018, Mookie Betts had a very special night in Toronto. The Sox were visiting the Rogers Centre. With an 81–34 record, the visitors were riding high. But this night, they lost to the Blue Jays, 8–5. Mookie singled to lead off and scored the first of two Red Sox runs in the top of the first. The Jays tied it. He came up again in the top of the second and tripled, also to left field, but was left stranded.

The Jays scored once in the second and once more in the third, and held a 4–2 lead when Mookie came up a third time, in the top of the fourth. This time, he doubled down the left-field line, but was again left stranded. Now he had a single, a triple, and a double in the game. All he needed was a home run for the cycle. Not that one can just conjure up a home run any old time; in fact, he was walked the next time he came to bat. The Blue Jays held an 8–4 lead after eight innings. In the top of the ninth, with one out and nobody on, Betts banged out his home run, but there was no other scoring for the Red Sox.

He clearly enjoyed the trot around the bases, though, knowing he'd accomplished something very unusual—something he had never done at any level. "I had plenty of guys letting me know what I needed. We had fun with it, but we were losing the game and I wanted to do what I could to win the game, so I was just trying to get on base."

When contemplating Mookie's future success, it should be said that there's nothing like healthy competition to spur a player to perform at his highest level (think Williams-DiMaggio or Jeter-Garciaparra). And for the Red Sox, of course, there's no better competition than the players in pinstripes. More specifically, it looks like Mookie and Aaron Judge are the new faces of the Red Sox-Yankee rivalry. Given their disarming smiles and laid-back personalities, it may not have the outward intensity of Carlton Fisk-Thurman Munson or Jason Varitek-A-Rod, but fans of each team don't care about such niceties. Heated arguments can be found on team sites across social media. What began with comparisons of Ted Williams and Joe DiMaggio and has included such pairings as Fisk-Munson, Mattingly-Boggs, and Garciaparra-Jeter is now a battle of right fielders.

A recent ranking by MLB's "The Shredder" promises to throw gas on the heated exchanges. In January of 2019, just as Mookie was finding a suitable place to display his 2018 MVP Award, The Shredder somehow concluded that Judge was the better player based on their data. Just to review, Mookie batted .346, hit 32 homers, and had a .438 on-base percentage. His Wins Above Replacement (WAR) was 10.9. Judge batted .278 with 27 dingers and a .392 OBP. His WAR was 5.5. Mookie also out-slugged the Gotham Goliath, .640 to .528.[125]

A Look Ahead to 2019

Throughout the 2018 season, Mookie batted leadoff for the Red Sox. In January 2019 it was determined that he would be moved to second in the lineup, behind Andrew Benintendi. Mookie was taken by surprise at the move but, ever the team player, accepted the switch without complaint. "[Alex] Cora hasn't put us in the wrong position yet so there's no reason to start questioning him now," he told Christopher Smith of *MassLive*. During a 35-minute phone conversation between the manager and the AL MVP, Cora laid out the reasons for the change. "He didn't just come without facts and stats and everything," Betts said. "That's why he's the best. Once he did that, I didn't say much but, 'All right. I gotcha.'"[126]

As an occasional number-two hitter, Betts had batted at a .304 clip with a .360 on-base percentage and a .430 slugging average (.790 OPS) in 150 plate appearances at that spot.

Benintendi was also open to the move. "I mean you've got the MVP and he's capable of driving in 100-plus," Benintendi said. "And I think maybe hitting me leadoff and hitting him second will give him more RBI chances and some more chances to drive in more runs. But I'm looking forward to it." He added, "I've hit lead-off before, and I'm going to try to set the tone like Mookie did last year," Benintendi said. "It'll be fun."

In limited action at the top of the lineup through the end of the 2018 season (97 plate appearances), Benny hit .322 with a

.381 on-base percentage and a .598 slugging percentage (.979 OPS). He also contributed five homers, seven doubles, and a triple. He promises that the transition won't cause him to change his approach at the plate. "It's essentially the same thing. You're just hitting first."

Brock Holt, Utility Player (and Honorary Killer B)

*He lacks the jutting jaw, the spotlight, and the swagger
but he has all the other attributes of the hero.*

When the regular third baseman is mired in a hitting slump and the Red Sox need a replacement, they have an "APP" for that. If the regular second baseman gets injured, they have an "APP" for that, too. In fact, they have an "APP" for virtually every position on the ballfield with the possible exceptions of catcher and pitcher. His name is Brock Holt and he's baseball's ultimate "APP"—All-Position Player.

It's a heroic-sounding name—Brock Holt. It suggests a swaggering star, a leading man, or perhaps an action hero with superpowers. He may be none of those things outside of Red Sox Nation, but to Red Sox fans, he's the Brock Star, the guy you call upon when one of the leading men is sidelined.

In the realm of superheroes, baseball's Brock Holt would be closest to Inspector Gadget and his gadgets are all baseball gloves of various sizes and styles: infield gloves, outfield gloves, first baseman mitts, and batting gloves. Holt has built a loyal following among Red Sox fans who recognize and appreciate his unselfish, blue-collar style of play. Like the legendary "fifth Beatle," he's more than earned the title of honorary fourth Killer B.

In just seven major-league seasons, the man they call "Brock Star" has played 25 games at first base, 183 at second, 123 at third, 53 at short, and 188 in the outfield (102 in left field, 12 in center, and 74 in right). In both 2014 and 2015, he filled in at seven different positions for the Sox. In 2016, he suffered a concussion early in the season and didn't return to the lineup until August 24, but still played at five different positions. In 2017, he was on the injured list for a large part of the season due to vertigo. In limited action he once again managed five positions. And in 2018, under rookie manager Alex Cora, he was used at six different locations on the field. The only roles he hasn't yet filled are those of pitcher, catcher, and batboy. Oh yes, he's also called on to DH on a regular basis. All of which is why he's been called the Swiss Army Knife of Major League Baseball and the most versatile performer since Sammy Davis Jr.

He's certainly the greatest Red Sox utility player since Billy Goodman, aka "the one-man bench." Like Holt, Goodman played every position except catcher and pitcher for Red Sox teams from 1947 to 1957. He was named to two All-Star teams and famously won a batting title (.354) in 1950 without a regular fielding position. That same year Goodman was runner-up for the MVP award.

Brock Holt would be a regular on many major-league teams, but it's the supporting role he plays on the Red Sox that makes him indispensable. When he subs for any one of the holy trinity outfielders, the transition is virtually seamless. Considering that two-thirds of that outfield own Gold Gloves and the other plays left field like no one since Carl Yastrzemski, that's impressive. Brock's lone error in 2018 came while playing shortstop. Along with his stellar defense, Holt's hitting is timely and his effort is all-out. Even the celebratory win-dance-repeat routines the Red Sox outfield trio once performed after victories didn't miss a beat when this versatile understudy filled in.

Holt is known as "the glue guy," as in the glue that holds a team together. The high value that major-league managers place on a prime, talented utility player such as Holt was evident when American League manager Ned Yost named him to the 2015 AL All-Star Game squad. Holt didn't disappoint. Coming into the game as a pinch-runner for Mike Trout, he promptly stole second, scored, and then stayed in the game to play left field.

Brock Holt was born in Fort Worth in 1988, making him the senior citizen (at age 30 after the 2018 season) when in the company of Bradley (28), Betts (25), and Benintendi (23). At 5-foot-10, he's more or less the same physical size as the others, although when weighed with their wallets, he's considerably lighter.

Holt's mother GayLynn knew that her son wanted to be a baseball player from the time he was six years old. "My mom's been a teacher, or counselor—high school counselor, elementary school counselor, teacher," says Holt. "She's been in the school system for a long time. She actually just recently retired. She helped a lot of kids. My dad worked as a distribution manager for Coca-Cola. He works in the oil business now. He's always been into cattle. We have land, raising cattle and selling them. That's his main love, owning land and raising cattle."

Brock wasn't likely to become a cowboy, preferring to flash the cowhide rather than roping the cow. "You ask anyone—from the time I was able to walk and talk, I just wanted to play baseball. I don't know why. I don't know why I started. I've always loved the game. But if I wasn't playing, I'd probably be doing something with baseball. Coaching, or something. I've always only wanted to do one thing so I feel blessed that I'm able to do that."

And he's done it at seven different positions.

Brock, who has an older brother, Garrett, and a younger sister, Shelby, went to high school in Stephenville, Texas, about 65 miles southwest of Fort Worth. He graduated from Stephenville High and then attended Navarro College in Corsicana for two years (where he hit .405 his sophomore year) before transferring to Rice University in Houston on a baseball scholarship. At Rice, he hit .348 and drove in 43 runs in 59 games. He led the team with 67 runs scored, stole 11 bases, and was named to that year's All-NCAA Regional Team.

It was in June 2009 that the Pittsburgh Pirates drafted Brock out of Rice. He was assigned to the State College (Pennsylvania)

Spikes in the New York-Penn League and played in 66 games in 2009, batting .299, with six homers and 33 RBIs. While he was with the Spikes, his father, Joel, and GayLynn often visited to watch him play. They also followed their son's progress through Internet broadcasts. On their 25th wedding anniversary they bypassed a romantic dinner at a fancy restaurant, opting instead to order takeout from Chili's because they didn't want to miss his game.[127] Ironically, Joel Holt played all the major sports growing up, except one—baseball. But he couldn't have been more supportive of his son's interest. It was Brock's grandfather, however, who gave Brock the best advice he claims he ever received. It was simple and more or less paralleled one of Ted Williams's "golden rules" of hitting; i.e., "Get a good pitch to hit." The grandfather's version was, "Don't strike at balls. Only strike at the strikes."

In 2010, Brock advanced to the Florida State League's Bradenton Marauders and, though he only got into 47 games due to MCL surgery, hit .351 with 27 runs batted in. Moving a rung up the ladder to Double-A ball, Holt played in 2011 for the Altoona Curve (Eastern League) and hit a solid .288 (.356 OBP) in 132 games. The minor-league homer he later said he was proudest of was the three-run round-tripper he recorded in that year's Double-A All-Star Game; Holt was named the game's MVP.[128]

He also started the 2012 season with Altoona, but spent the month of August in Triple A with the Indianapolis Indians. There he hit an impressive .432 in 24 games and earned himself the proverbial September call-up.

His big-league debut with the Pirates came on September 1, 2012. He played in 24 games for Pittsburgh and hit .292 in 72 plate appearances. Interestingly, the only position he played was second base, but it was in his short time there that he picked up the nickname "Brock Star." As fate would have it, the Red Sox were looking to strengthen their bullpen and had their eyes on Pirates reliever Joel Hanrahan. A deal was struck on December 26, involving six players. On the recommendation of Red Sox scout Nate Field,

Holt was packaged with Hanrahan and thus became a member of the Red Sox organization.

When he arrived in spring camp, he soon became friends with Jackie Bradley Jr. "I didn't really know what to expect," he recalled. "I met Jackie first. That was the year that he just went bananas in spring training. He had a great camp. He was the talk of the camp the whole time. Me and Jackie have been friends since day one. We've got a lot in common. I'm happy he's on our team, that's for sure. He's one of the best outfielders I've ever played with and got to watch play."

Even today, Holt remains impressed with Jackie's anticipation: "His jumps and his reads are so good. He'll make the diving catch but he only dives when he has to. A lot of catches that some center fielders make diving, he makes them standing up. He gets such good reads. You watch him. When the ball's hit, he puts his head down and turns around and catches it. It's impressive."

Holt started the 2013 season in Pawtucket, but cracked the Red Sox lineup on June 6, playing primarily at third base. In 11 games that July, he had eight RBIs.

Every year since, he's made at least one side trip to Pawtucket (in 2018, it was only one), but the bulk of his playing time has been with the Boston Red Sox, and he's got two world championship rings as a result. He didn't actually play in the postseason for the 2013 world champions but saw playoff action in 2016, 2017, and 2018.

Brock is the ultimate team player, the ultimate teammate, and he loves the game of baseball, and the Red Sox. "I wouldn't want to be anywhere but right here, doing what I'm doing, getting to put on this uniform every day and play for this organization," he said in January of 2019. "It's something that you can only dream about and I'm getting to live it every day."[129] That kind of loyalty is rare in today's game and is one of the reasons for his large fan base. Based on a very unscientific study of fan apparel at Fenway, he may hold the record for "Most Player T-Shirt Sales by a Part-Time Player."

In 2014, Brock first experienced playing outfield in the majors. "I was just kind of thrown into the outfield. It was just one of those things where we had some injuries. I was moving around, playing different positions and doing pretty well. They just asked if I could go out there and try it out, and I did. John Farrell, the manager at the time, pulled me into the office and he told me to get some reads in the outfield.

"You use a bigger glove out there and so he wanted me to get some reads, just in case. It turned out I played an actual game in the outfield about a week later."

His resume of "previous" positions continued to expand. In addition to playing 44 games in the outfield, he was used 39 times at third base, including in Mookie Betts's debut game. Two days later, on July 1, Holt was in left field, Jackie was in center, and Mookie was in right. And the Three Amigos were together for the first time. It was also the first time he had met Mookie, since Betts had been in minor-league camp that spring. But he was impressed from the very beginning. "From the moment I saw him, I said, 'He's going to win MVP one day.' I didn't think it would take very long. He's a special player who can do everything on a baseball field. He's fun to watch."

Brock was part of the original outfield configuration that started doing the win-dance-repeat routine in the spring of 2016. "I don't know how it started," he says. "Chris Young was part of it. And then Benny came up and became a part of it. I think it was kind of just like a mutual thing. It was one of those things like, 'What shall we do when we win? The outfielders have got to do something.' It was just one of those things. Let's do something where we meet up in center field. I think it just kind of evolved into what it became. It started out as just doing a little dance and that's it. And then it got to 'let's take a picture of the player of the game in the outfield.' And then the player of the game has to do his own little thing. It got to be pretty popular. It was just to have a little fun."

Fred Lynn knows the value of a player with Holt's unique skill set. "I absolutely love that guy," said the popular member of the Red Sox Hall of Fame. "He can fill in anywhere and he has some pop in his bat. He can do it all like Cesar Tovar [a player in the 1960s and '70s, mostly for the Minnesota Twins, known for his versatility]. I don't know how he learned to play all those positions, but they are so lucky to have a guy like that on the team. We didn't have that luxury when I played."

That's pretty much what Tim Hyers said, recalling the season he was interim hitting coach for the Red Sox after Greg Colbrunn suffered a midseason brain hemorrhage. "Brock was a 2014 All-Star. We called him the Brock Star. He'd never played the outfield and yet he's flying around all over the outfield. We plugged him in left and he made some great catches, and I remember Butter [coach Brian Butterfield] and those guys saying, 'Hey, can you play center?' 'Well, yeah, I'll try,' he said. And he went out and played center. He played right, and obviously he played the infield. He just made a name for himself. He was breaking up double plays. Hustling to first. He's just a tough out.

"From a hitting coach's perspective, he helps this team a lot because he will grind a pitcher down. If you don't throw him a strike, he's going to be at first base because he ain't going to expand. He ain't going to swing at balls. He's going to walk. It's so hard. You've got to throw pitches in there, and then he's got a really good swing. He puts the ball into play, hard. He makes it really difficult for a pitcher. You have to make pitches to get him out. He does so much to help a team. He's not going to get the headlines in the news, hitting homers all the time. He just makes it really difficult for the opposing pitcher to get through the inning because it's, 'Here comes Brock.' You've still got to make quality pitches.

"It's amazing what he does coming off the bench. He's got a swing that's low-maintenance, which is perfect for coming off the bench, and it's so consistent. He knows his principles, how to get himself ready to play. He's got his routine down. To me, he's just so underrated for the things that he does for the club—in so many different ways—offensively, defensively, and with his baserunning. He's a solid piece of the team who gets overlooked because we have so many who get the headlines. I was so happy for him hitting for the cycle. He's a tough out and if you let up, he's just going to lace one.

"Remember the Philly game, when he came up against [Tommy] Hunter, their middle reliever? The game was just kind of going along and then Brock Holt pinch-hits [in the top of the eighth, on August 14, 2018]. Hunter tried to sneak a fastball by him and—bam! A homer. We win the game. It's just so hard to do what he does, though, not playing for three or four days and then coming in and facing the best relief pitching in the game. He comes in and gives you a quality at-bat. You have to have self-confidence to do that. You have to be relentless. You've got to have that edge."

Brock Holt's Game-Winning Hits and the Biggest Days of His Career

Brock Holt's Red Sox career began on July 7, 2013. He'd been traded by the Pirates the day after Christmas in 2012 and played in Pawtucket until called up. Perhaps the ideal utility player, as of the beginning of the 2019 season, he owns a career .336 on-base percentage (.267 batting average) with precisely 2,000 plate appearances since his debut on September 1, 2012. He's driven in 175 runs and scored 245 runs in his 552 games. And consider where he has played:

LF: 102 games
CF: 12 games
RF: 74 games
1B: 25 games
2B: 183 games
SS: 55 games
3B: 123 games

About the only thing it seems he hasn't done is pitch and catch his own pitches in the same game, à la the classic Bugs Bunny cartoon.

In 297 chances as an outfielder, he has been charged with only two errors, for a .993 fielding percentage.

Like Bradley, he has two world championship rings. Unlike Bradley, Betts, and Benintendi, "Brock Star" does have a game-winning hit in postseason play. More precisely, he has a game-winning plate appearance. It wasn't a base hit. It was a bases-loaded walk off Lance McCullers in the top of the seventh inning in Game Four of the American League Championship Series. The date was October 17, 2018. His walk produced the seventh run of the game, which Boston won, 8–6.

Other game-winning hits in his career:

April 19, 2014: His triple in the seventh broke a 2–2 tie and beat the A's at Fenway.

May 31, 2014: His second-inning two-run homer off Tampa Bay's Jake Odorizzi gave the Red Sox a 2–0 lead in a game they won, 7–1.

July 9, 2014: His first walk-off! Daniel Nava had doubled in Betts to tie the White Sox, 4–4. Holt singled in Nava to win it.

April 14, 2015: Holt grounded out to shortstop in the bottom of the seventh, but it was a productive out that scored the run that ultimately won a one-run game.

April 24, 2015: A three-run homer in the top of the eighth at Camden Yards. Sox win, 8–5.

June 26, 2015: Top of the 10th single at Tropicana. Sox win, 4–3.

September 16, 2015: A single in the top of the third, at Camden Yards again, scored Jackie Bradley Jr. for the second run of a runaway 10–1 Red Sox win.

April 5, 2016: A single to left off Corey Kluber in the top of the sixth at Cleveland drove in Hanley Ramirez and was the game-winner. Three days later, he had one of those days—five RBIs including a grand slam. The Sox couldn't have won the 8–7 game without him, but the game-winner was not his.

May 5, 2016: A third-inning sacrifice fly won this game in Chicago: Red Sox 7, White Sox 4.

May 9, 2016: Holt's two-run homer off Fernando Rodriguez in the bottom of the fifth provided the margin that made all the difference.

July 19, 2016: The first run of the game was Holt's home run to deep right-center field in the bottom of the third. Rick Porcello and four relievers shut out the Giants.

August 4, 2016: In the top of the 11th in Seattle, Holt beat out an infield single to the shortstop and Travis Shaw managed to score from second base with the go-ahead run.

August 29, 2016: At Fenway, Holt's double to deep right-center in the bottom of the fourth gave the Red Sox their fifth run of the game. As the final score was 9–4 over the Rays, it was Holt's hit that won the game.

September 23, 2017: Holt missed a considerable amount of the 2017 season, struggling with vertigo. He had just seven runs batted in on the season, and the one game-winner he had was an odd one. In Cincinnati's Great American Ballpark for a late Saturday afternoon game, he was the second batter up in the game. Xander Bogaerts led off with a double to left. On a passed ball, Bogaerts took third base. Holt then hit a sacrifice fly to center, scoring the X-Man. The Red Sox shut out the Reds, so that was the run that won the game.

April 17, 2018: In Anaheim, a simple single to left in the top of the second drove in the second run of the game in a 10–1 triumph. Holt added two more runs batted in later in the game.

June 3, 2018: On a Sunday night in Houston, it was his two-run triple off Charlie Morton in the top of the sixth that won the game for the Red Sox.

June 11, 2018: The game in Baltimore was scoreless for 11 innings. Then came the top of the 12th. With nobody out, the Red Sox loaded the bases. Back-to-back sacrifice flies by Holt and Bradley gave the Red Sox two runs, one more than they needed.

August 14, 2018: Playing in Philly, the score stood 1–1 after seven. Pinch-hitting for starter Rick Porcello, Brock Holt strode to the plate, facing Tommy Hunter. He swung at the first pitch and hit it out to right-center. No more Philly runs scored, Holt's hit won the game, and Porcello pocketed the W.

August 18, 2018: It was the bottom of the first inning. The Red Sox had already scored two runs. The bases were loaded with just one out. Holt hit a grounder to first base. Rays first baseman Jake Bauers threw wildly to the plate. Holt reached on the error but the third and fourth runs scored on the play in the eventual 5–2 win.

September 11, 2018: This one was legit. A three-run homer deep down the right-field line in the bottom of the seventh won the game against the Rays, 4–2.

September 15, 2018: Bottom of the fifth with the Mets in town and the Fenway stands a little awash in orange and blue. It was 3–1, Mets, but then JBJ doubled to tie it and—after an intentional walk to Devers—Holt doubled, too, to make it 5–3, the final score.

October 17, 2018: And let's not forget this game, detailed earlier.

Brock Holt's Biggest Day

There can't be much doubt about this one. When you do something that's never been done before, and it's in the glare of the postseason spotlight, on national TV, it's a tough act to follow. Brock's biggest day was in Game Three of the American League Division Series, October 8, 2018. Playing against the New York Yankees, the first game of the series played in New York, he had five RBIs. He singled leading off the fourth inning and, later in the same inning, hit a two-run triple. He added an RBI double in the eighth, and he came to the plate in the top of the ninth inning lacking only a home run for the cycle. No batter in major-league history had ever hit for a cycle in postseason play. Austin Romine, a backup catcher, had taken over on the mound for the Yankees with the Red Sox leading, 14–1, and retired the first two batters on groundouts. Then he walked Ian Kinsler. Holt hit the first pitch into the right-field seats—a two-run homer, which put the Red Sox ahead, 16–1.

Holt described the experience in refreshingly frank and honest terms. "I knew I needed a home run. I told everyone, 'Get me up. I need a home run for a cycle.' I was going to try to hit a home run, but I figured I'd ground out to first, be out in front of something. But I scooted up in the box a little bit, and I was going to be swinging at anything . . . I was trying to hit a home run. That's probably the first time I've ever tried to do that."[130]

Brock Holt's First Cycle

It wasn't the first time Holt had hit for a cycle. The first time was back on June 16, 2015. The Atlanta Braves were back in Boston, playing in the same ballpark where they had won the 1914 World Series (as the Boston Braves.) Leading off, Holt doubled high off the left-field wall off Braves righty Julio Teheran. Mookie Betts followed with another double, and the Sox had themselves a quick run.

He grounded out in the third, then lined a single to right in the fifth. In the bottom of the seventh, he hit a solo home run off the beleaguered Teheran, another opposite-field drive to left field, caroming off the Monster seats and dropping onto the field. Boston had a 6–2 lead.

The triple, of course, is the most difficult of the four hits to get, but in the bottom of the eighth inning, Holt came up again— and tripled. He hit the ball over the center fielder's head. It hit the dirt of the warning track and bounced high in the air, deep enough that he reached third base with a perfunctory pop up slide. "Obviously, I knew I needed a triple," he said after the game. "I didn't expect to hit one. But as soon as barrel hit ball, I thought, *Oh, my God.*"

The Sox won the game against the Braves, 9–4. Holt's cycle was the 20th in Red Sox franchise history. Bobby Doerr was the only player who had done it twice.

The authors of this book told him we found it refreshing that— needing only a home run to complete his second cycle—he went for it, and didn't dissemble later, saying that he was just looking to get on base. He acknowledged that he was going for it.

"Yeah, I was trying. I was trying. I'd never really done that, but why not? The game's out of hand. We're feeling pretty good about where we're at. It was just one of those things. There was a position player [Austin Romine] on the mound, so you knew you weren't going to get anything funky. He was going to try to throw a strike. Yankee Stadium's a good place to try to hit a homer out, with that short right-field porch. That was very cool."

There are four major-league players who have hit for three cycles. We can hope that one day soon, Brock will become the first "tricyclist" in a Red Sox uniform.

An Integral Part of the Team

In 2017, Brock had a tough time with recurring vertigo and was limited to 64 games. But in 2018, he contributed big time, appearing in 109 games. "It was good. I was healthy this year, he explained. "I feel like, when I'm healthy, I can help. I had a rough couple of years prior. I didn't know if I would ever be able to perform like I knew I was capable of performing. The issue was mostly with my vision. I didn't have a whole lot of dizzy spells. It was mostly my vision. I wasn't able to lock in like I needed to. But I was healthy last year [2018] and felt great."

Holt first met Andrew Benintendi in August 2016 when Benny was first called up and in a reversal of roles, the soon-to-be left-field fixture was able to play left field in order to give utilityman Brock time to get healthy again.

Brock has become a unique and ubiquitous player for the Red Sox. It's a role that has earned him two world championship rings to date, and a role he embraces. "It's something I've kind of become accustomed to over the years, just being ready to play wherever I'm needed. It's something that I enjoy doing. It's given me a chance to be a big-leaguer and play for this team, and be a part of this organization. I'm grateful for that."

Brock Holt has been an integral part of the Red Sox for six seasons now. With second baseman Dustin Pedroia out for almost all of 2018, Holt played 79 games in the infield, mostly at second base, and only 16 in the outfield. He stays close to his outfield partners, though, and is always available on short notice.

"We're all close," he said. "The good thing about this team is that everyone gets along. Everyone roots for each other. I spend more time with Benny than anyone else. Me and him kind of hit it off right from the beginning. We sit next to each other on the plane. Me and him and Mitch [Moreland], we'll go to breakfast together on the road. Benny's a real good friend of mine. I love Jackie and Mookie, too. That's the special thing about this group is that there's really no cliques. We're all in it together. There's a lot of good dudes on this team."

After the 2018 season, Brock and his wife Lakyn decided to stay in Boston for the winter, along with their son Griffin. "We still have our home in Texas, and we spend some time there, too," he said in March 2019. "But Boston is kind of a comfort thing for us. We like our home and the city and people. It fits us."[131] They've put down roots in the community, perhaps none more meaningful than in his work with the Jimmy Fund, the children's cancer center that was adopted as an official Red Sox charity back in 1953. Since 2014, Brock has been Red Sox Jimmy Fund Co-Captain. He welcomes patients and groups to games each week and visits the Clinic when he can. Lisa Scherber, the Dana-Farber director of patient and family programs, known affectionately as The Play Lady for her own ability to connect with kids, told Chad Jennings that Brock was an all-star in that department as well.[132]

The term *utility man* has somehow become synonymous with "bench player" or "second stringer." Holt has helped to restore and rehabilitate the job description and redefine a role whose dictionary definition has never changed: Useful, beneficial, effective, valuable. We'd ask Mr. Webster to add to that list the word *indispensable.*

The Killer B's as a Team

Despite their individual achievements, the Killer B's as a whole (a swarm?) present the greatest force to be reckoned with. It's in considering how the three truly complement one another that it becomes clear how they became the Killer B's.

Threats on the Basepaths

It's one thing to get on base, but the ultimate goal is to advance around the bases and ultimately score. The Red Sox have become more of a baserunning team in recent years—in part because they've got the talent that they can use to advantage.

Consider these numbers:

2, 8, 3, 9, 8, 17

7, 21, 21, 26, 30

1, 20, 21

Those three lines signify the number of stolen bases by each of the three Red Sox outfielders, for the years they've played for the Red Sox. The first line is JBJ's, the second is Mookie's, and the third is Benny's. Each of the three achieved new highs in 2018 (the final number of stolen bases on each line).

Outfield coach Tom Goodwin (also the first-base coach) works with the Sox on their baserunning. He had served as the baserunning-outfield coordinator in the team's minor-league system from 2009 to 2011, and first got to know Jackie and Mookie late that year when he worked with them at instructional league in Fort Myers in the fall of 2011. Since his arrival in 2018, Goodwin had kept his eyes on the two Red Sox outfielders.

"I'd been watching from afar," said Goodwin, "checking out the highlights and always seeing these guys. I'd already known the talent that JBJ had, but Mookie was still in the infield when I left. But watching him over the last two or three years, you could just see the talent that he had."

One thing the three did was get on base. In each of his five full seasons, Mookie Betts has worked to earn even more bases on balls:

21, 46, 49, 77, 81.

As a trio, they drew 198 walks in 2018.

The Red Sox as a team stole 125 bases in 2018. And the three guys who stole the most bases were Mookie (30), Benintendi (21), and Bradley (17). The next closest was Xander Bogaerts with eight. In other words, the three outfielders each stole at least twice as many bases as anyone else on the team. Bradley had more or less doubled the number he'd swiped in any previous year, a fact that Goodwin wishes was better known.

"Jackie's not one to come out and say something like that," he says. "He came to us and said, 'I know I could steal more bases.' And A. C. [Alex Cora] being the way he is, made it clear. He said, 'We're going to run. If we can, we're going to run. So let's just be ready to do it if the opportunity presents itself.' And that's basically what we were trying to do.

"You're not going to go out there and try to steal 200 of them but you're going to take what the other teams are going to give you. It gives you a little advantage."

"We try to make guys aware of pitchers' tendencies and maybe catchers' tendencies, and everybody took it to heart. It wasn't just them. They might have had more opportunities to run, hitting in the top of the order. Jackie's down at the bottom with those guys coming up—or at least he was last year. There were just good running times for us to go.

"Jackie was kind of the one who we knew could steal more bases than he had in the past. And not only *could* he do it. He *wanted* to do it. That helps out a lot. A lot of guys come in the spring and say, 'Hey, this is what I want to work on. I want to get better at this.' But if they don't put the effort in to get better, then it's probably not going to happen. Jackie really did. We would come out early—[bench coach] Ron Roenicke, myself, and Jackie—and we would just sit there and talk about some of the things that he'd like to do. Ron had some very informative things to say about how we're reading pitchers and when you might want to take off for second base. There was a lot of information. He didn't have to take it all. You're not going to take it all in, but you take what you need and whatever you don't need, you filter it away for another day in case it comes up. Jackie did an outstanding job of just picking the pitchers to run on, picking the pitches to run on. Hopefully we can do some of that as well this year."

Despite the increased number of attempts, Jackie was caught stealing only once in 2018. Goodwin chuckles as he takes the blame for that one blemish on an otherwise perfect record of thievery.

"He only got caught one time, and that was probably my fault because . . . actually, it *was*," he says sheepishly. "It was a time I should not have sent him. It was real close at second base, still. They reviewed it. He was really trying to get to where he didn't get thrown out and stole 20 bases. It was one of those things where they knew he was running."

Tom brought one big advantage to the equation. He'd been taught by one of the master basestealers of all time, former Dodgers great Maury Wills. And the philosophy was not just stealing bases but being aggressive on the basepaths in general, pushing the envelope when possible, and eventually coming around to score. Fans watching the Red Sox soon noticed the change. They seemed to be a little better at going first to third, or scoring from second base on a single. And then there were those special times when the opposing team put on a shift and had no one playing near third base, so even a steal of second could result in a quick pop-up slide, with the base thief then running on to an inadequately defended third base. It takes a certain attitude.

"It goes back to the attitude where you're always looking to get that extra 90 feet," explains Goodwin. "That's what we try to teach. We're not satisfied with just the first 90 feet. We're always looking to take that next 90. We make the opposing team stop us from doing that. We're always looking for the one base beyond the base that we know that we have. I try to teach those guys that, because I learned that from Maury Wills when I was coming up with the Dodgers. He'd say, 'Goody, you know you've got second base, but we're always looking for third. We're always looking for that 90 feet past the 90 feet that we know that we have.'"

Thus, there was only one degree of separation from Maury Wills to the three Red Sox outfielders.

"It was pretty special to have a guy like that teaching me," admits Goodwin before invoking the name of the most celebrated single-game base stealer in Sox history. "I know Dave Roberts had some of the same kind of teaching from Maury, because we were with the Dodgers at the same time. It shows in the managing; A. C. [Alex Cora] came up with the Dodgers as well. I know he learned a lot from Maury."

Among the three of them, the outfielders scored 308 runs for the Red Sox in 2018.

Their Defense Never Rests

"Chris Sale said the outfield of the Boston Red Sox makes you feel like there's four of them out there."
–Ron Darling, after Game Four of the 2018 ALCS

The best defensive outfield in baseball? It sure felt that way for fans of the 2018 Red Sox.

One game alone—Game Four of the ALCS in Houston—featured three plays that most fans won't soon forget. First there was the ball José Altuve hit in the bottom of the first inning that would have been a great catch by Mookie Betts, or a home run, but turned out to be neither. Umpire Joe West made the call of fan interference (replays clearly showed a fan brushing Mookie's glove closed so the ball bounced off it, rather than land in it). Altuve was called out. (In the bottom of the sixth inning in Game Five, Alex Bregman hit a ball to right that was almost a carbon copy of Altuve's drive, but this time the fans backed away from any possible interference and Mookie make the catch.)

Then, in the bottom of the eighth, leadoff batter Tony Kemp hit a line drive into right field that Mookie chased down and grabbed before it made it into the corner. In one smooth motion, he picked it up and—without even setting himself—fired a perfect strike to Bogaerts, who put the tag on Kemp at second base and turned a near-double into an out. The very next inning, the Astros were down by two runs with two outs. The bases were loaded on three walks by Craig Kimbrel. Alex Bregman hit a ball to left field that Andrew Benintendi ran to, dove for, and snagged with a head-first sliding catch just before it hit the grass. Video replay of the grab is surely in heavy rotation on Red Sox fans' playlists.

Statcast™ provided some on-screen measurements. There had been 32 seconds of "opportunity time." Benintendi had to cover 45 feet to catch the ball. The probability of him making the catch was declared to have been just 32 percent. And yet he made the catch.

Little wonder that Red Sox fans felt they had the best outfield in baseball. But is there a way to try and pin a feeling down? How can one attempt to measure differences in fielding ability?

They're talented defenders, for sure. Are they more than that? Among the best?

In 2018, both Betts and Bradley were awarded Gold Gloves and Benintendi was listed as one of two runners-up to the Royals' Alex Gordon. For Betts, it was the third Gold Glove he has won in as many years. For Bradley, it was his first. Benintendi's rookie year was 2017, so it was only his second major-league season. Based on his stellar play, he could be next to earn the gilded mitten.

The Red Sox scouting and baseball operations departments both play a huge role in the overall defensive strategy. When a new batter approaches the box, you'll occasionally see one of the out- fielders pull a little card from his hip pocket, consult it, and then shift position, moving a little more to the left or the right, com- ing in a little or backing up a bit. There are catches made in every game that look routine, but really only look that way because of pre-positioning information that indicates the best place to stand on the field for each individual batter. If you're standing closer to where the ball might more likely be hit, there is less distance to travel in order to field the batted ball.

Cheat sheets aside, the players still have to make the plays.

First, let's look at a few traditional measures of fielding from the 2018 season.

Player	Fielding %	Chances	Errors	Assists
Benintendi	.984	257	4	12
Bradley	.982	341	6	9
Betts	.996	280	1	7

Clearly, Mookie had the highest percentage and was only charged with one error all season long. But Benintendi had quite a few more assists, throwing runners out.

That said, there are a lot of variables to consider when it comes to fielding acumen. How to measure the variables involved and try to determine the best fielders? It's a question that has challenged some of the best minds currently studying baseball. One attempt to codify measures is the SDI (SABR Defensive Index.)[133]

In 2018, for the sixth consecutive season, the SDI was used to help select the winners of the Rawlings Gold Glove Award and Rawlings Platinum Glove Award™, presented by SABR. The SABR Defensive Index accounts for approximately 25 percent of the

Rawlings Gold Glove Award selection process which are added to the votes from the managers and coaches.[134]

The SABR Defensive Index draws on and aggregates two types of existing defensive metrics: those derived from batted ball location-based data and those collected from play-by-play accounts. The three metrics representing batted ball data include *Defensive Runs Saved* from Baseball Info Solutions, *Ultimate Zone Rating* developed by noted sabermetrician Mitchel Lichtman, and *Runs Effectively Defended* based on STATS Zone Rating and built by SABR Defensive Committee member Chris Dial. The two metrics included in the SDI originating from play-by-play data are *Defensive Regression Analysis*, created by committee member Michael Humphreys, and *Total Zone Rating*.[135]

Overall, the top five rankings in 2018 for the three outfield positions were as follows:

Left Field:		
Alex Gordon	KCR	11.0
JaCoby Jones	DET	6.9
Justin Upton	LAA	6.6
Andrew Benintendi	BOS	4.0
Marwin Gonzalez	HOU	3.3

Center Field:		
Delino DeShields	TEX	6.2
Mike Trout	LAA	4.2
Jackie Bradley Jr.	BOS	3.9
Adam Engel	CHW	2.9
Kevin Pillar	TOR	2.3

Right Field:		
Mookie Betts	BOS	12.8
Aaron Judge	NYY	8.7
Max Kepler	MIN	7.8
Mitch Haniger	SEA	4.7
Kole Calhoun	LAA	4.3

Only the Red Sox and the Angels had a top-five fielder at each position. Looking at the outfield as a whole, the gap between Betts and Calhoun in right field gives the Red Sox outfield the edge. Mookie Betts had the highest rating of any outfielder at any position.

The influence of SDI in the final voting for the Gold Gloves has been seen over the six years that SDI has been provided to the voters prior to their balloting. In the first year, there was about a 40 percent alignment between top SDI ranking and ultimate Gold Glove recipient. Through both refinements of the five metrics comprising the SDI and the reputation SDI has built among the electorate, that alignment is now closer to 90 percent.

The position one plays, and the ballpark in which one plays his home games, matters a lot. Benintendi doesn't have nearly as much ground to cover in Fenway Park, as does either of his fellow outfielders. But he's much more likely to have to field a ball off a wall—The Wall, in his case. The Green Monster. That he had 12 assists shows he's got a good arm, but may also reflect the fact that baserunners who try to grab an extra base haven't yet fully appreciated that arm.

Dwight Evans, for instance, had 14 to 15 assists in 1975, 1976, 1978, and 1979. In 1980, it was 11, and then the next four years were all in single digits. He wasn't necessarily a better fielder in the years he had 15 than in the year he had six or seven, but rather that runners had learned to respect his arm and thus didn't challenge him as much.

Good communication skill is another important quality of a good fielder.

As Goodwin said, "I didn't know personally how good these guys were because I hadn't been around them in so long. You knew the talent was there, but I didn't know what kind of players they were. But when I came over and was able to see the communication and just how these guys really wanted to get after it in the outfield—and then you throw Andrew Benintendi in there—it was something special that we had from the git-go."

He was particularly taken with how well they feed off each other.

"Oh, it's beautiful. It is beautiful to watch. As good as the corner guys are—Mookie winning Gold Gloves and Benny's younger, running around out there—they both want to be like Jackie. Any time they're comparing themselves to something, they'll say, 'Yeah, but I can't do it like Jackie.' That's what I love to hear. Jackie's not going to say that about himself. He just goes out and gets his work in. He just stays ready to play every day—which all of them do—but to hear them say, 'I wish I could do that like Jackie does it,' is music to my ears, because as good as those guys are, they're still trying to get better. And that's what it's all about."

As has been pointed out, all three of the K B's were at one time center fielders, spending a significant amount of time at that position in the minors and/or at the college level as well as in the big leagues. Benintendi played 24 games in center field in 2018 alone. As Fred Lynn has indicated (see foreword), it's a decided advantage to have guys who have center-field talent be able to help you out with the other positions, too. Goodwin agrees with Lynn's conclusions.

"Without a doubt," he says. "You know guys are going to need days off. You're not going to have [another] Jackie Bradley out there when someone takes his place but when you have those other two guys available, at least it's pretty close. You're not giving up a whole lot—but you are giving up something! Anytime Jackie's not out there, let me tell you—you're giving something up, man. It's not easy to replace a guy like him."

Goodwin explains that the challenges involved in playing center field require unique skills and extended everyday experience. As a result, adjustments from the left- and right-field positions are not easy to make. Even Benny and Mookie can't make the transition seamlessly.

"The thing is that when you have a guy who's used to playing the corners, and he's playing center field now, you don't get the same communication as far as you're going to go get the ball.

Center fielders have to go get the ball. It's up to the other outfielders to look around and see if that guy's going to be there or not. A center fielder's trained to go to his left, trained to go to his right, trained to go back. . . . So sometimes we don't get that same aggressiveness from Benny or from Mookie when they're in center field, because they're not used to taking charge like that."

Of course, another outfield weapon that Goodwin has at his beck and call is Brock Holt. Goodwin mentioned the intangibles he brings to the table. "He's another 'B,' right? Brock's another Killer B. Brock is that guy that you need on a team. He kind of loosens things up when things might not be going the way that you want them to go. He'll step up . . . not trying to be a clown or make a mockery out of the situation, but he's that guy who will keep everybody up, keep everybody positive on the bench. And then, obviously, when his time comes to do some damage, he does that as well."

Brock played 11 games in right field in 2018. "That's the kind of guy he is. You can put him anywhere—anywhere—and he's going to give you a solid, solid effort. He played a solid outfield for us this year."

Tom is quick to spread the credit between the instincts of the three outfielders, the communication that exists between them, and the team's analytics staff, which helps them plan.

"There's an advance meeting. It goes over where we're going to play guys. This is what we're thinking. Why we're playing guys this way. We don't get in too much depth, as far as me being the outfield coach going to Dana [pitching coach Dana LeVangie] and talking to him about how they're going to pitch, but the [analytics] guys who are putting this together kind of already know the guy pitching and how he's going to pitch. A lot of it is done by the analytical team. They did a great job for us this past year. This is the first year I got a chance to work with these guys and they did an outstanding job.

"It's not just telling a guy where to play, because sometimes that doesn't work. There has to be some kind of explanation of why. Guys want to understand it, and as coaches we want them to understand it—so they can give 100 percent knowing that we've done all that we can do as far as research to put us in the best position to make a play. . . . But there's still some old school left in there because our guys at time will go, 'You know what? I know our sheet has us playing one way, but this guy looks like he's trying to do something absolutely different at the plate right now, so we're going to move on this other side.' We give them that freedom to do that"

Of course, the art and science of playing outfield still involves a lot of traditional strategies and first-person observations, intangible nuances, and experience-based instincts that analytics can never provide. For example, the outfielders aren't really able to pick up the signals the catcher gives the pitcher, but they can still learn a lot from watching activities at home plate.

"They can watch [opposing batters'] swings," says Goodwin. "They can see what this guy's trying to do with his swing, if he's trying to go to the opposite field, or if it looks like he's trying to hook the ball. That's really what they look for from the outfield. And how the foul ball is coming off. If he's fouling balls off and Mookie's playing him in the right-center field gap but he's fouling balls off down the right-field line, Mookie will tell Jackie, 'Hey, I'm going to move over a little bit.' Maybe he'll move accordingly, or maybe he'll stay there, but he'll know that Mookie's moved so now if the ball is hit in that gap, he knows he'll have to go and get it."

The Best Outfield in Baseball?

In 2018, Bradley and Betts both won Gold Gloves, and Benintendi came in second among left fielders. But those who feel badly for Benny need not worry; his self-worth isn't suffering. He's happy to be part of a classic outfield. "Honestly, these guys don't go out and play for that," says Goodwin. "They just want to go out and make plays. They want to make plays for their team so their team has the best opportunity to win that game on that given day. Benny's no different." Goodwin paused, and added, "Obviously, it would have been nice to have a three-position sweep. Maybe we'll work on that this year."

When asked if the Benny-Jackie-Mookie outfield is the best in baseball as of 2018, Goodwin replied cautiously.

"It was a really good one. I'm not going to be that guy who comes out and says 'best here, best there,' because you just never know, but it's a really good outfield. We're very fortunate as Boston fans and for the Boston organization to have those guys out there and to watch them play the way that they play together. It's just a joy to watch. It's just fun to come to the stadium and watch these guys play every day. I've got a front-row seat for it."

Tom added that when he first came over from the Mets he hadn't known what kind of men the Red Sox outfielders were. He now respects them even more as people than as players.

"They're really . . . they're good guys. Nothing against anyone I've coached in the past, but when it's fun to come to the ballpark every day, because of the guys you have on the team—and the guys are as good as they are—it's an extra bonus to have the types of human beings that those three guys are."

Whether the Killer B's outfield will be considered one of the greatest of all time is impossible to predict. Longevity, luck, and numerous other factors must come together before any such judgement is made. And if heart plays much of a role in these matters of fate, their odds go way up. Regardless of what happens, this outfield has the attention of all of baseball, and Red Sox fans can't wait to see their fortunes play out over years to come. Will Jackie start to hit more consistently? Will Benny win a Gold Glove? Will Betts stay in Boston?

The last word on the subject goes to Boston Red Sox hitting coach Tim Hyers.

"These guys do a lot of things to help you win. I look at them that way. They can beat you in a number of ways. They can beat you with power. They can beat you with defense. They can beat you with baserunning. They can beat you throwing on the basepaths, using their arms. And they're not afraid of the moment—every

single one of them. You can go back through the 2018 season and
see it. Jackie had so many incredible catches, saving you a game.
Then you get Mookie jumping over the fence making that play in
the playoffs and you can see him throw out his buddy at second
base in Houston [Tony Kemp] from down the line. That's one of
the best throws I've ever seen, in a key moment of a game. Take
Benintendi's diving, laying-out catch.

"You can pick out some better tools in different packages, but
for guys who can beat you in a number of ways—we saw it all last
year—those three are probably at the top of my list. All three can
beat you in a number of ways!

"They're so consistent with their work ethic. Benny will be in
the cage—you can mark his time, well before three o'clock. Jackie's
there and he's got his routine. And Mookie's one of the hardest
workers around. It's fantastic—their passion to win and help the
team. They're just pros. They prepare themselves. They're ready.
As a coach, it really makes it fun and easy to work with them. You
just know they're into their team and into winning."

Epilogue

B aseball is all about arguments and opinions and disagreements. They feed and nourish our national pastime. That's one of the things that makes it such a great game and why a knowledge of the past enriches the experience for fans. Seen in a vacuum, the Killer B's are just another pretty good major-league outfield. We can admire their skills and cheer them on, but we really don't know how good they are unless we can compare them with some of their predecessors.

For some, that opportunity to compare comes with very little effort via something known as the aging process. All you have to do is wait, live a reasonably long life, and you will automatically start saying, "Yeah, he's good but remember (fill in the player's name)?" Or "Sure, he's got a gun for an arm, but you should have seen the throw to the plate that (fill in player's name) made in the (fill in the year) World Series." Those of us in this category are blessed to have seen Willie Mays's slashing style in the outfield and on the basepaths, standing out in every year's All-Star Game as if he were surrounded by mediocrity. Or Sandy Koufax, the southpaw who for five years was virtually unhittable. Or Ted Williams, who was the greatest hitter since Babe Ruth. Or Hank Aaron, who quietly and courageously broke Ruth's home-run record.

The thing is that when Hammerin' Hank stood at 713 homers, human curiosity practically forced you to the library (this was the seventies after all, and therefore pre-Google) to look up this Babe Ruth guy. Once you knew what the Bambino had done, Aaron's accomplishment grew in stature. And you also learned a little bit about American history, about the color barrier and the integration of baseball, and other historical facts that put Aaron's home run feat in greater context.

It's human nature for young people to believe that everything is at its apex of excellence right now, at this particular point in human history. The music is the best, the movie stars are the best, and so on. Nostalgia for the past requires that you have a past and young people can't be blamed if they think that Chris Sale is the greatest pitcher of all time, or Mike Trout the greatest player. But remember, some day in the not too distant future, there will be people 15 or 20 years your junior who will be convinced that the greatest outfield in history is the one currently playing for the (fill in the team). These people may well be your own sons and daughters. You will argue, of course, and caution them that there were some pretty good ones back in 2019, but your case may fall on deaf ears. That's the beauty of baseball. The record books are there for all to see and in many cases so is the video and audio. Do yourself a favor and learn about baseball history. Your enjoyment of the game will increase 100 percent.

Benny, Jackie, and Mookie deserve to be compared with the great outfields of the past. Failing to make those comparisons does them a disservice. As the Old Perfessor, Casey Stengel, once said, "You could look it up."

Afterword by Bob Costas

Bob Costas is the best Commissioner of Baseball we never had. Articulate, knowledgeable, and steeped in the history of baseball, his greatest qualification for that position may be his genuine and abiding love of the game. If you doubt it, ask him if you can see the Mickey Mantle card he still carries in his wallet.

Each of them—Benintendi, Bradley, and Betts—is good enough to play center field and all three are Gold Glove-caliber right where they are. They could conceivably sweep all three outfield Gold Gloves some year.

Benintendi is Boston's best at playing the wall at Fenway since Yaz. He's a player of consistent All-Star quality—a very good outfielder and a good baserunner who can swipe 25 or 30 bags a year, and a dangerous hitter with 30 HR/ 30-plus doubles power.

Bradley is already one of the game's best outfielders, with tremendous range and leaping ability. At the plate, you wonder when he will put it together. His play in short stretches during the 2018 postseason may have provided a glimpse. Right now he strikes out too much and doesn't get enough hitter's counts. He needs to bunt and spray the ball around to utilize his speed as a way to snap out of slumps. He's got a good attitude and that increases the chances that he will figure it out.

Betts is a delight to watch. He plays the game with joy. Over the last few seasons, he's been one of the top two players in the game, along with Mike Trout. A classic five-tool guy, Betts runs, fields, throws, hits for average, and hits for power. He's a natural leader and a smart player. He makes spectacular plays, but also important ones that are sometimes overlooked, like cutting balls off to hold doubles to singles and playing caroms cleanly. He seldom, if ever, throws to the wrong base. The big question long-term is can Boston make him a Red Sox for life.

If these three stay healthy and remain in the fold, Boston will have baseball's best outfield for several seasons to come.

Thanks and Acknowledgments

Fred Lynn—author interviews, February 14, 2019 and February 23, 2019

Diana Collins—author interview, January 10, 2019

Chris Benintendi—email exchange, January 29, 2019

Tom Goodwin—author interview, February 16, 2019

Brock Holt—author interview, January 17, 2019

Tim Hyers—author interview, February 16, 2019

Ray Tanner—author interview, January 16, 2019

Thanks to Kevin Gregg and Daveson Perez of the Boston Red Sox.

Thanks to Kent Reichert of the University of South Carolina for supplying Jackie Bradley Jr.'s complete college stats.

Endnotes

1 Jeff Sullivan, "The Red Sox Do Have An All-Time Outfield," https://blogs.fangraphs.com/the-red-sox-do-have-an-all-time-outfield/#more-297976 October 18, 2018.

2 Chad Jennings, "Carl Yastrzemski Looks at This Red Sox Outfield and Sees A Group for the Ages," *The Athletic*, March 7, 2019.

3 Ibid.

4 Correspondence with Steve Andrews, January 27, 2019.

5 Eric Olson, "Hogs' Benintendi": 'I Like It A Lot' on TD Ameritrade Park," Associated Press, *Baton Rouge Advocate*, June 13, 2015: 28.

6 Julian Benbow, "Red Sox May Consider Look at Papelbon," *Boston Globe*, August 14, 2016: C6.

7 Peter Abraham, "Benintendi Came Long Way in Short Time," *Boston Globe*, October 10, 2016: C2.

8 Ibid.

9 Peter Abraham, "In Retirement, Ortiz Keeps Close Eye on Red Sox," *Boston Globe*, December 3, 2016: C2.

10 Peter Abraham, "Betts Won't Get Carried Away," *Boston Globe*, February 14, 2017: D4.

11 Peter Abraham, "A Labor of Glove," *Boston Globe*, February 19, 2017: C1.

12   Dan Shaughnessy, "Next Big Thing," *Boston Globe*, March 26, 2017: C1.

13   Nick Cafardo, "Not Squared Away," *Boston Globe*, May 19, 2017: C1.

14   Dan Shaughnessy, "Benintendi: Striking Resemblance to Lynn," *Boston Globe*, August 13, 2017: C1.

15   Peter Abraham, "Social Media Keeps Them Engaged," *Boston Globe*, March 25, 2018: S6.

16   Peter Abraham, "Plans Are in Place To Get Sale Back Up to Speed," *Boston Globe*, September 29, 2018: C2.

17   A. J. Perez, "Four-Hit Night Puts Andrew Benintendi in Rare Air with Red Sox," *USA Today*, October 24, 2018.

18   https://www.mlb.com/news/andrew-benintendi-wins-ap-play-of-the-year/c-302160108

19   Christopher Smith, "Andrew Benintendi: Boston Red Sox Star Ranks Postseason Catches, Best Parade Sign; Talks About Showing Emotion & Signing 'Maybe a Couple Thousand' Photos," *MassLive.com*, February 26, 2019.

20   Alex Speier, "In More Ways Than One, Andrew Benintendi Prefers the Direct Route," *Boston Globe*, April 12, 2017.

21   https://www.mlb.com/news/andrew-benintendi-father-have-strong-bond/c-236712760

22   Alex Speier, "In More Ways Than One."

23   Ibid.

24   Ibid.

25   Christopher Smith, "Jackie Bradley Jr.'s Mom Almost Miscarried Future Boston Red Sox Outfielder; 'Then I Was in Labor With Him for 19 Hours'," *MassLive.com*, May 3, 2018.

26   Ian Browne, "Bradley's Character Stems from Father," *MLB.com*, June 18, 2016.

27   http://www.legacy.com/obituaries/progress-index/obituary.aspx?n=william-m-saye&pid=153015394

28   Jonathon Seidl, "The Pro Baseball Player Who Isn't Afraid to Die," *Iamsecond.com*, July 5, 2016.

29   Christopher Smith, "Jackie Bradley Jr.'s Mom."

30   Ibid.

31   Christopher Smith, "Boston Red Sox's Jackie Bradley Jr. Is Very Laidback Unlike His Mother, a Former State Police Officer," *MassLive.com*, May 14, 2015.

32   Author interview with Ray Tanner, January 16, 2019.

33   Dan Roche, "Jackie Bradley Jr. Maintains Strong Bond With Cape League Host Family," June 10, 2016. https://boston.cbslocal.com/2016/06/10/red-sox-jackie-bradley-jr-cape-cod-league-host-family/

34   Peter Abraham, "Getting A Little Extra Out of Crawford," *Boston Globe*, August 9, 2012: C11.

35   Christopher Gasper, "Bradley Catching Fly Balls and Eyeballs," *Boston Globe*, March 6, 2013: C1.

36   Peter Abraham, "Mishap Humbles Brentz," *Boston Globe*, March 16, 2013: C6.

37   Dan Shaughnessy, "Rookie Brings Fresh Life to New Season," *Boston Globe*: A5.

38   Ron Chimelis, "Boston Red Sox Rookie Jackie Bradley Jr. Never Imagined the Delightful Dilemma He's Created," March 28, 2013, *MassLive.com*, https://www.masslive.com/redsox/index.ssf/2013/03/boston_red_sox_rookie_jackie_b.html

39   Peter Abraham, "Bradley is Poised As Slump Lingers," *Boston Globe*, April 13, 2013: C1.

40   Peter Abraham, "Red Sox Are Hoping No. 7 is Lucky for Them," *Boston Globe*, June 4, 2013: C3.

41   Peter Abraham, "Let's Get It Started," *Boston Globe*, October 6, 2016: D1.

42   *Boston Globe*, February 8, 2014 Peter Abraham, "Bradley Welcomes Sizemore Signing," *Boston Globe*, February 8, 2014: C1.

43   Stan Grossfeld, "Is There Really Crying in Baseball?," *Boston Globe*, March 3, 2014: C5.

44   Peter Abraham, "A Winning Proposition," *Boston Globe*, June 11, 2014: C3.

45 Peter Abraham, "Slumping Bradley in a Funk," *Boston Globe*, August 7, 2014: C5.

46 *Ibid.*

47 Peter Abraham, "Workman Ready to Resume Role," *Boston Globe*, June 27, 2014: C3.

48 Jim Prime and Bill Nowlin, *Amazing Tales from the Red Sox Dugout* (New York: Sports Publishing, 2017), 29.

49 Ben Coles, "I Can't Imagine Playing for Five Days'—Red Sox Star Jackie Bradley Jr. on Cricket and Facing the Yankees," *The Telegraph*, December 28, 2018.

50 Nick Cafardo, "Investments Paid Off with Castillo Signing," *Boston Globe*, August 24, 2014: C9.

51 Peter Abraham, "Sox Hope Outfield Issues Have Been Tracked Down,", *Boston Globe*, January 12, 2015: C1.

52 Alex Speier, "Red Sox Use Neuroscouting on Prospects," *Boston Globe*, February 19, 2015: D4.

53 Peter Abraham, "Bradley Doing His Level Best to Stick with Red Sox," *Boston Globe*, March 6, 2015: D3.

54 Peter Abraham, "Red Sox' Bradley Has Hit on a Solution," *Boston Globe*, September 4, 2015: D4.

55 Nick Cafardo, "With Betts Secure, Bradly in Limbo," *Boston Globe*, May 15, 2015: D5.

56 Ibid.

57 Nick Cafardo. "In Bradley's Case, Slumps Are Excused," *Boston Globe*, September 20, 2015: C4.

58 Nick Cafardo, "Red Sox Have No Shortage of Story Lines," *Boston Globe*, February 7, 2016: C4.

59 Christopher Gasper, "Bradley's Prospects Are Better," *Boston Globe*, March 3, 2016: D2.

60 Peter Abraham, "Work Force," *Boston Globe*, May 20, 2016: D1, D7.

61 Sam Galanis, "Jackie Bradley Jr. Admits He Didn't Feel Like Part of a Team Until 2016," *NESN.com*, 2016, January 18, 2017.

62   Peter Abraham, "Work Force," *Boston Globe*, May 20, 2016: D7.

63   Peter Abraham, "In This Together," *Boston Globe*, July 8, 2016: D1, D5.

64   Peter Abraham, "Bradley Has Set Goals for Season," *Boston Globe*, February 5, 2017: D3.

65   Ibid.

66   Peter Abraham, "Sox' Bradley Counting on Improvement," *Boston Globe*, March 30, 2017: D4.

67   Chris Mason, "Enough Already, Give Bradley Jr. Gold Glove," *Newburyport Daily News*, August 21, 2017.

68   http://soxprospects.com/players/bradley-jackie.htm

69   Chris Mellen and Bret Sayre, "The Call-Up: Jackie Bradley Jr.," *Baseball Prospectus*, April 1, 2013.

70   Christopher Smith, "Jackie Bradley Jr.'s Mom."

71   Matt Desrosiers, *bostonsportssyndicate.com*, February 28, 2019.

72   Peter Abraham, "His Work Continues on Revamped Swing," *Boston Globe*, February 7, 2019: D5.

73   Ibid.

74   Joe Posnanski, "JBJ and What Should Be Baseball's 'Last Error'," *MLB.com*, August 16, 2018.

75   Chris Mellen and Bret Sayre, "The Call-Up: Jackie Bradley Jr." *Baseball Prospectus, April 1, 2013.*

76   Joe Posnanski, "JBJ and What Should Be."

77   Peter Abraham, "Dombrowski Pouts Lots of Value on Bradley," *Boston Globe,* November 16, 2017: C4.

78   Dan Shaughnessy, "Seasoning Enhances Bradley," *Boston Globe*, February 18, 2018: C6.

79   Ian Browne, "JBJ Makes 'Unreal' 103.4 mph Throw to Nab Runner," *MLB.com,* June 20, 2018.

80   Julian Benbow, "Bradley Serves Up the Catch of the Day," *Boston Globe*, May 29, 2018: C5.

81   Bob Ryan, "Numbers Can't Measure Their Worth," *Boston Globe*, August 5, 2018: C6.

82   Chad Jennings, "For Jackie Bradley Jr., Breaking in a New Mitt a True Labor of Glove," *The Athletic*, February 27, 2019.

83   Dan Shaughnessy, "Clout Made Noise in Statement Game," *Boston Globe*, October 17, 2018: C1.

84   Alex Speier, "Red Sox Patience Was Rewarded by Bradley," *Boston Globe*, October 20, 2018: C1.

85   Author interview with Ray Tanner, January 16, 2019.

86   Greg Hadley, "Before he was World Series MVP, Steve Pearce Deferred MLB Dream for South Carolina," *The State* (Columbia, South Carolina), October 30, 2018.

87   Julian Benbow, "This Prospect is One Sure Betts," *Boston Globe*, June 6, 2014: C6.

88   Jen McCaffrey, "The Story of Mookie Betts' Rise from Nashville to Boston Red Sox Franchise Cornerstone, *masslive.com*, July 15, 2015.   https://www.masslive.com/redsox/index.ssf/2015/07/boston_red_sox_mookie_betts.html

89   Joe Rexrode, "The Mookie Betts Story, Starring Nashville and Strong Parents," *Tennessean*, October 12, 2018.

90   Tom Huddleston, Jr., "Red Sox Star Mookie Betts Was Too Small to Make a Little League Team—so His Mom Started Her Own," *www.cnbc.com*, October 23, 2018.

91   Ian Browne, "Betts Inherited Baseball Acumen from Dedicated Mom," MLB.com, May 8, 2015.

92   Gary Phillips, "From Little League to Boston, Mookie Betts' Mom Has Never Stopped Coaching Him," *The Sporting News*, May 13, 2018.

93   Ian Browne, "Betts Inherited Baseball Acumen."

94   Gary Phillips, "From Little League to Boston."

95   Jessica Camerato, "Childhood Accident Put Things in Perspective for Mookie Betts," *Boston.com*, September 11, 2014.

96   Tom Verducci, "Moveable Beast," *Sports Illustrated*, June 1, 2015.

97   Jessica Camerato, "Childhood Accident."

98   Ibid.

99   Brian MacPherson, "There's Nothing 'Light' About Mookie Betts' Future," *Providence Journal*, April 4, 2015.

100   Alex Speier's article provides a wealth of details on Mookie and neuroscouting. Alex Speier, "Red Sox Use Neuroscouting on Prospects," *Boston Globe*, February 19, 2015: D4.

101   Christopher Smith, "How Mike Trout, Mookie Betts Went Overlooked but Not by Red Sox, Angels and Examining the MLB Draft's Complexity," *MassLive.com*, February 13, 2017.

102   Bill Koch, "Red Sox Notes: Jackie Bradley Jr. Regains Spotlight," *The Telegram*, October 19, 2018.

103   Alex Speier, "Red Sox Patience Was Rewarded by Bradley," *Boston Globe*, October 20, 2018: C1.

104   See Kevin Thomas, "On Baseball: Mookie Betts's On-Base Streak Ends," *Portland Press-Herald*, May 14, 2014.

105   Ibid.

106   *The Tennessean*, February 24, 2010 and February 23, 2011.

107   McCaffrey, op. cit.

108   Julian Benbow, "For Betts, Difference is Striking," *Boston Globe*, April 25, 2014: C10.

109   Eric Wilbur, "Red Sox Find A Mixed Bag in Betts' Much-Hyped Debut," *Boston.com*, June 30, 2014.

110   Nick Cafardo, "Much Excitement as Mookie Betts Makes Debut," *Boston Globe*, June 30, 2014.

111   Scott Lauber, "Mookie Betts' First Homer Caught by Former Tennessee Summer League Opponent," *Boston Herald*, July 3, 2014.

112   https://www.bostonglobe.com/sports/2014/06/05/red-sox-prospect-mookie-betts-calmly-succeeds-every-level/Dznk0U6bjOo1vQFBpXAmQI/story.html

113   Nick Cafardo, "Team Success Counts in Awards Voting," *Boston Globe*, October 2, 2016: C8.

114   Peter Abraham, "Betts Second Best," *Boston Globe*, October 20, 2018: D1.

115   Alex Speier, "Betts Embracing Status in Baseball," *Boston Globe*, March 23, 2017: D1.

116   Alex Speier, "Data Driven," *Boston Globe*, September 30, 2018: C1.

117   Alex Speier, "Incredibly, Betts Just Keeps Raising Game." *Boston Globe*, July 17, 2018: D3.

118   Nick Cafardo, "Betts Still Second to None," *Boston Globe*, August 4, 2018: C1.

119   Owen Pence, "Betts Not Ruling Out Playing Some Second," *Boston Globe*, October 21, 2018: C12.

120   Rob Bradford, "The Story Behind Mookie Betts' Good-Luck Necklace," *weei.radio.com*, May 6, 2018.

121   Ibid.

122   Hayden Bird, "Mookie Betts Surprised A Group of Nashville Children By Giving Them Bikes," *Boston.com*, December 14, 2018.

123   Joe Rexrode, "Why Mookie Betts is the Tennessean Sportsperson of the Year for 2018," *The Tennessean*, December 28, 2018.

124   Eduardo Gonzalez, "Dad's a Dodger, but Joe Kelly's Son Is Still a Mookie Betts Fan and He Lets the Whole Clubhouse Know It," *Los Angeles Times*, March 14, 2019.

125   Alex Speier, "Sox' Cast Remains the Same, but Will It Follow a New Script?", *Boston Globe*, December 15, 2018: C1, C5.

126   Christopher Smith, "Mookie Betts New Boston Red Sox No. 2 Hitter after More Than Half Hour Phone Call with Alex Cora," *MassLive.com*, January 29, 2019.

127   https://www.collegian.psu.edarchives/article_4d621c9f-72ec-5b17-93f2-bee565a4e4b9.html

128   http://www.espn.com/blog/boston/red-sox/post/_/id/39972/20-questions-the-legend-of-brock-holt

129   Justin Leger, "Brock Holt Continues to Embrace Role on Red Sox," *NBC.com*, February 17, 2019.

130   Peter Abraham, "Relentless Sox Do a Number on Yankees," *Boston Globe*, October 9, 2018: C4.

131   Peter Abraham, "Holt's Ties to Boston Stronger, Invaluable," *Boston Globe*, March 2, 2019: B1.

132 Chad Jennings, "With the Kids of the Jimmy Fund, Brock Holt Finds His Calling, and a Home," The Athletic, December 20, 2018. https://theathletic.com/724574/2018/12/20/with-the-kids-of-the-jimmy-fund-brock-holt-finds-his-calling-and-a-home/

133 To learn more about the SABR Defensive Index, visit SABR. org/SDI.

134 Rawlings announced the revised selection process overview in March 2013 at the annual SABR Analytics Conference as part of its new collaboration with SABR. Since that announcement, SABR enlisted an independent committee of experts in baseball analytics and defensive measurement to devise the SDI. The SABR Defensive Committee includes:

- Committee chair Vince Gennaro, SABR president and author of *Diamond Dollars: The Economics of Winning in Baseball*
- Sean Forman, founder of Baseball-Reference.com
- Ben Jedlovec, MLB's Director of Engineering, Data Quality
- Chris Dial, author and recognized expert on defensive metrics
- Michael Humphreys, author of *Wizardry: Baseball's All-Time Greatest Fielders Revealed*
- F. X. Flinn, SABR Board of Directors

135 Within SDI, the three measures based on batted-ball data are accorded somewhat more weight than the data based on more traditional measures, such as outfield assists. DRS and RED are each weighted at 25 percent, UZR is rated at 20 percent, and TZR and DRA are both weighted at 15 percent.